Cooking in Cast Iron

COOKING IN

CAST IRON

YESTERDAY'S FLAVORS FOR TODAY'S KITCHEN

MARA REID ROGERS

HPBOOKS

HPBooks
Published by The Berkley Publishing Group
A division of Penguin Putnam Inc.
375 Hudson Street
New York, New York 10014

First edition: September 2001
Published simultaneously in Canada.

Visit our website at
www. penguinputnam.com

Library of Congress Cataloging-in-Publication Data

Rogers, Mara Reid.
Cooking in cast iron : yesterday's flavors for today's kitchen /
Mara Reid Rogers.
p.   cm.
Includes index.
ISBN 1-55788-367-X
1. Cookery, American.   2. Cookware.   3. Cast iron.   I. Title.

TX715 .R7259   2001
641.5'89—dc21
00-066358

PRINTED IN THE UNITED STATES OF AMERICA

10 9 8 7

CONTENTS

ACKNOWLEDGMENTS

With great appreciation to Bob Kellermann, president of Lodge Manufacturing Company in South Pittsburg, Tennessee, for the gift of some of their premium cast-iron cookware to help me test the many recipes in this book.

INTRODUCTION

. . . a well-seasoned iron pot or skillet is impossible to beat for creating exotic flavors in many homecooked meals. While other cookware strives to leave no taste in food, the iron pot, when properly seasoned, will instill a distinctive flavor that becomes richer . . . over many years of use.

The South Carolina Wildlife Cookbook

THE BENEFITS OF CAST-IRON COOKWARE IN THE MODERN KITCHEN

A cast-iron skillet tells a story. Cast-iron cookware, in general, possesses an inherent romance that no other cookware has. It is heirloom cookware. Oftentimes, home cooks inherit cast-iron pots and pans from their parents, grandparents, or great-grandparents. Whether inherited or newly purchased, advanced and novice cooks alike fall in love with cast-iron cookware because it fulfills their tastes and needs. It definitely seems that nothing tastes better than when cooked or baked in a well-seasoned cast-iron skillet or pan, and certainly nothing cooks better.

There is no substitute for a cast-iron skillet; no pan has as many uses. I believe it is the most valuable and versatile tool in the kitchen. Of course, there are many recipes in the following pages using other cast-iron utensils, too, such as the Dutch oven. But if you just own one cast-iron skillet, you can make the majority of the recipes in *Cooking with Cast Iron*. Never in a cookbook have you been able to cook and bake so much with just a skillet. Cast-iron cookware is the world's most perfect and versatile cookware and will always be a kitchen essential because it is indispensable for quality cooking.

Cooking in Cast Iron is for the bare, unfinished type of cast-iron cookware/bakeware, not the enameled cast iron. One of the many advantages "regular" cast-iron cookware has over enameled is that enamel gets stained and chipped. Also, enamel prevents the formation of a properly seasoned cast-iron surface, which is the only nonstick coating that will last.

With *Cooking in Cast Iron* in hand, you will never be at a loss for enticing recipes that maximize this cookware's amazing potential. The beauty of this cookware is its relevance to today's cooking because cast iron does it all, from quick sautéing or frying to low-temperature, long, slow braising, simmering, or poaching to baking. A cast-iron skillet is great for dry-toasting nuts and seasonings as well. It is also ideal for browning foods such as vegetables and poultry, searing meat prior to roasting, and Cajun-style blackening.

Can you make the recipes in this book with cookware made from another material? Well, yes, but why would you want to? If you don't have the cast-iron pot or skillet and must use another type, don't change the ingredients, just know that you'll have to add a little more cooking or baking time to the recipes you choose, because they are written for cast iron, and cast iron cooks faster. In general, I find that cast iron cooks and bakes 10 to 15 minutes faster than other cookware materials, but that is merely a starting point. Follow the "watchwords" or doneness tests in each recipe, such as "when a toothpick inserted in the center of the cake comes out almost clean with a few moist crumbs clinging to it," as guidelines to monitor the adjustment of the cooking and baking timing if you use a different cookware material with these recipes, and you'll be fine.

Because of its history, timelessness, versatility, reliability, and numerous culinary benefits, cast-iron cookware is the one type of cookware that has a direct link to our past and a firm hold on our future. In essence, cast-iron cookware has the flavor of nostalgia for the way we eat today.

Cooking in Cast Iron begins with a nostalgic excursion into America's culinary past and continues into our modern-day kitchen through a "melting pot" of diverse and unique recipes inspired by different American cultures and utilizing a wide variety of ingredients and techniques. With an eye for taking what's best from the past and present and adapting it for the future, this cookbook offers the bountiful, varied, and distinctive flavor of America's culinary landscape, cast-iron style.

This is food at its best—not fancy, but simple to cook, with complex and vibrant flavors. There is no better-tasting food. *Cooking in Cast Iron* provides a sampling of dynamic American cuisine, and through these recipes, aims to capture, preserve, and celebrate an all-important part of our history and history-in-the-making.

WHAT MAKES CAST-IRON COOKWARE SUPERIOR TO OTHER COOKWARE?

- Cast-iron cookware is both flameproof for the stovetop and ovenproof for the conventional oven—so you can go from stove to oven and vice versa. But be aware that the handle(s) will be hot—always use potholders.

- Cast-iron cookware is not only pleasing to the eye, it can be taken from stovetop or oven directly to the table for ease of entertaining.

- Once seasoned, cast iron is naturally nonstick and can be used over extremely high heat, which you can't do with the majority of nonstick cookware because the nonstick coating tends to burn.

- Once it has been seasoned, cast-iron cookware can be used with very little liquid or fat. Some chefs and home cooks use none at all.

- Cast iron heats quickly and evenly, which saves energy.

- Cast iron is dark and porous, enabling it to absorb more heat than other cookware. It absorbs heat evenly; conducts and retains (holds) the heat very well, giving the home cook more control; and results in more quick and efficient cooking.

- Cast iron is not only excellent for stovetop cooking, it is also excellent for baking. The material of choice for discerning bakers, cast iron is the original nonstick bakeware.

- Because cast iron absorbs heat evenly and conducts and retains heat well, it gives an even-temperature bake, with no hot spots that result from temperature fluctuations in your oven. Cast-iron bakeware tends to produce a crisp exterior yet tender interior.

- Cast-iron cookware is easy to clean and season (see page xiv).

- Cast-iron cookware is extremely durable and will last for centuries—not just one lifetime, but several lifetimes. Cast-iron cookware doesn't just grow old, it grows better. It *improves* with age.

- Cast iron is inexpensive, a good value for the money, and readily available. Previously owned pieces can be acquired for pennies at flea markets and antique shops. New ironware made in the old style, as well as new pieces such as woks, are extremely affordable and can be purchased at stores and through mail order.

- Cast-iron cookware is available in a variety of shapes and sizes for a multitude of culinary uses, for both general culinary techniques and specialized tasks. Here's a *partial* list of what's available: skillets, Dutch ovens, casseroles, griddles, popover pans, corn stick pans, grill pans, woks, fluted cake pans, muffin pans, French bread pans, and bread stick pans.

- Cast-iron items are available in a wide range of sizes. There is even cookware large enough for large-batch cooking to feed twenty or more (in other words, a small army). Cast iron's weight is another virtue; it will never tip over!

- Cast-iron cookware can be used over a variety of heat sources, from a conventional stovetop and oven to a wood-burning stove to a fireplace (hearthside cooking) to a pit or open fire such as a campfire.

C AST-IRON FACTOIDS

- During the past ten years, the sales of cast-iron cookware have risen from $20 million to $34 million, which indicates that *a vast number* of cooks are purchasing cast-iron cookware.

- Columbus brought cast iron with him to the New World in 1492.

- Cast-iron skillets are born one at a time, each in a different sand mold.

- Lewis and Clark carried cast-iron cookware on their expedition to the Pacific Northwest in 1804.

- The early explorers traded European cast iron for furs from American Indians.

- Iron pots and skillets were considered part of the "crown jewels" by England's King Edward III, who reigned from 1327 to 1377.

- Paul Revere is credited with the design of the pot that became known as the Dutch oven. The cast-iron Dutch oven is the original slow-cooker.

THE RUGGED AND ROMANTIC HISTORY
OF CAST-IRON COOKWARE

Lewis and Clark carried cast-iron kettles on their 1804 expedition to the Pacific Northwest; and gold miners not only cooked dinner in their Dutch ovens, they used them to pan for gold.

Molly Culbertson, *Country Home*, October 1990

America grew up on cast iron. Cast iron is Americana; it has been a part of America since its beginning and was part of the settlement of this country. Whether it's the brawny, rough-hewn, newly purchased cast-iron piece or the silky-smooth patina of an aged piece, each holds memories, memories of a time long ago. Cast-iron cookware graced the hearths of the colonial settlers. Then, cast-iron skillets, the basic black pot, the kettles, the spider of colonial times, and Dutch ovens crossed the prairies with the pioneers traveling the American West, a rugged lifestyle that involved campfires and cast iron. The various international backgrounds of these generations of adventurers of the West helped flavor the cast-iron "pot." Into this "pot" went new, Western regional ingredients, along with recipes and flavorings from the migrants' homelands. Through innovation and improvisation and a need for simple, hearty fare to be cooked over open fires, the people who settled this country's western regions developed a unique style of cooking as they conquered the land. Cast-iron cookware was a tool for a cultural link that helped develop American cuisine as we know it today.

Wake up, Jacon, day's a-breakin'

Fryin' pan's on an' hoecake bakin'.

Bacon in the pan, coffee in the pot.

Git up now, and git it while it's hot.

Traditional cowboy song

As the United States continued to grow, each immigrant group that arrived added some part of its heritage. These influences, in addition to a blending of cooking traditions, recipe-swapping as Americans became more mobile and traveled the United States and other countries, and the media and publications, further broadened the scope of our cuisine into the melting pot it is today. All the separate parts are fused to make a whole that continues to grow.

> # **H**OW CAST-IRON COOKWARE IS MADE
>
> The Lodge Company, the largest maker of iron cookware, warms the iron to a free-flowing orange-yellow 2,800 degrees Farenheit, and pours it into sand from northern Mississippi. From the sand emerges the classic skillet shape: a pure circle, a little pucker for pouring, and a straight handle . . .
>
> Phil Patton
>
> *Esquire,* November 1990

HOW TO CARE FOR YOUR CAST IRON: SEASONING AND CLEANING

Please don't get the impression that cast iron is temperamental. It's not. It just needs proper care and seasoning, and then it will reward you with years of service and give you something to pass on to future generations.

SEASONING (CURING)

In addition to seasoning, general care of cast-iron utensils is important. The steps are very simple and don't take long, and the steps are the same no matter what piece of cast-iron cookware it is. "Seasoning" and "curing" are words used interchangeably to mean the same thing in relation to cast-iron utensils: It is the process of allowing oil to be absorbed into the iron, creating a nonstick, rustproof finish. Cast-iron cookware will turn black, smooth, and fairly shiny with accumulative use; these are the visual signs that it's seasoned well. The pores of the iron will be sealed, providing a durable coating that helps to prevent sticking and rusting.

The fastest way to cure cast-iron cookware to the deep black "seasoned" patina is to deep-fry in it; the hot oil cures the cookware quickly. Because this is not practical for everyone to do, the following is the more typical route.

All new cast-iron cookware must be seasoned prior to use. And periodically, you may want to re-season it. The method always stays the same. With proper curing (seasoning), your cast-iron cookware will last for many years.

First, peel off and discard any labels. Wash thoroughly with mild dishwashing liquid, rinse with hot water, and dry thoroughly with a kitchen towel. Never allow cast-iron cookware to air dry, and never wash it in the dishwasher.

Next, spray or use a paper towel to wipe a thin, even layer of vegetable oil cooking spray (with no flavorings or salt added), vegetable oil, or vegetable shortening over the entire surface—the inside and the exterior—including all corners, edges, and lids, rubbing it in, and wiping away any excess. This is an important step because otherwise there will be a fat buildup and the cast iron will smoke when used. It will also smoke when other fats, such as margarine or butter, are used (however, I find bacon drippings work well).

Finally, line the bottom of the oven with foil (to catch any drips) and preheat to 350F (175C). Place the utensil upside down (to prevent the oil from building up inside the cookware) on the center oven rack and bake for 45 minutes to 1 hour to cure (season). Turn off the heat and allow the utensil to cool naturally in the oven to room temperature. Remove from the oven and wipe off any excess oil with a paper towel.

The deep black, fairly shiny patina of properly cured (seasoned) cast-iron cookware may take years of use to develop, so you will not see that surface color yet. However, the cookware is now ready to use or store for future use. You should use your cookware often, because it's the cooking, and proper care and seasoning, that perfects the surface.

CLEANING

After each use, you must clean, wash, dry, and re-rub with fat for proper care.

Never put cast-iron cookware in the dishwasher; it must be hand washed.

Many folks never let their cast-iron piece even come into contact with soap; they simply rub it clean with salt, rinse it, and proceed with the drying and seasoning steps, whether for use or storage. If they are camping, and if they don't carry a small container of salt in their backpack, the classic choice is sand (which is used in the birthing process of cast-iron pieces).

Always clean the utensil immediately after each use (be careful if the utensil is still hot) with mild dishwashing liquid and water (never scour with abrasive detergents) and dry thoroughly with a kitchen towel. Never soak or allow to air dry, or the cast-iron will rust. Never use a metal scouring pad or metal brush. Instead, use a stiff, nonmetal scouring pad or brush to remove any stubborn food particles. Then repeat the seasoning process given above. The cookware is now ready to use again or store.

STORING

Place a clean, dry paper towel flat on the inside of the cookware to absorb any moisture and help prevent rust, and store in a dry place. Always store with the tops or lids off so moisture won't collect inside.

RUST SPOTS

All unseasoned utensils will rust. Rust spots, stuck-on food, a metallic taste, or discolored foods are signals of inadequate or improper seasoning or may result from cooking highly acidic foods. If this occurs, wash thoroughly and re-season according to the directions given earlier in the "Seasoning" section.

If your old or new cast-iron utensils develop light rust spots, scour (with a stiff, nonmetal brush) the rusty areas very gently with a light touch until all traces of rust are gone. Then rinse, dry, and repeat the process as directed in the "Seasoning" section.

COOKWARE TYPES

Although the skillet, Dutch oven, corn stick pan, muffin pan, and loaf pan are some of the most popular cast-iron cookware/bakeware items, there are so many other utensils that are handy to have in your kitchen.

There are new items on the market, such as the wok and fajita pan. There is also the ridged cast-iron grill pan. It's great for low-fat cooking and is perfect for city-dwellers who dream of grilling but don't have the space. It is also terrific for anyone who wants to grill on a rainy day.

Some of the more unusual, specialty items include waffle irons, toasters, deep-fryers, and pie irons. Altogether, there are too many items to list here, but half the fun of cast iron is in the exploration. As you start to scout for both brand-new and aged, heirloom pieces via mail order, the World Wide Web, garage sales, auctions, and antique stores, you'll be able to add to the list yourself. Be on the lookout for those pieces that are no longer manufactured, and before you know it, you may have a collection.

RECIPE POINTERS

When following those recipes that call for heating oil or melting butter in a cast-iron utensil prior to beginning the cooking process, always swirl the skillet or other cookware item so that the oil or butter coats the interior of the skillet evenly.

In any recipe that calls for canned beef or vegetable broth, if you make a rich homemade beef or vegetable broth, by all means use those instead.

I have developed the recipes in this book under the assumption that you will only use properly seasoned and cared-for utensils. This is especially important, because you will get a metallic flavor and/or discoloration to your foods if the cookware item is not properly seasoned. In addition, I have used techniques and carefully proportioned ingredients and ratios so that you avoid cooking highly acidic mixtures in cast iron. Highly acidic mixtures will react with cast iron by giving a metallic flavor and discoloring under the aforementioned circumstances and, at times, on their own even in a properly seasoned item if they have a chance to break down the cured surface of the item. Because highly acidic foods damage the seasoning of the cast iron, never marinate food in cast iron. And do not let food stand in it for a long period of time, always transfer any leftovers to a bowl before refrigerating.

The first few times you cook with a new piece that was just seasoned, cook food with as little water content as possible and avoid acidic foods (since they have a tendency to remove the seasoned surface). For the first few times of use, it is best to cook foods that are high in fat, such as sausage or bacon. Also, uncover hot foods when you remove the utensil from the heat; the steam can also remove the protective seasoned coating.

Because cast iron heats evenly, you will not need to use extremely high cooking temperatures. Start with the medium to medium-high setting. Cast iron works well on lower temperatures, too.

Uneven and/or intense heating may cause the utensil to crack or warp. When using any utensil larger in diameter than the diameter of the burner, it is best to preheat the utensil in the oven, then slowly bring the utensil up to cooking temperature on the burner.

BEEF, PORK, AND LAMB

Beef and Barley Stew
with Roasted Garlic

CHEWY, NUTTY BARLEY IS OFTEN overlooked by chefs; however, I believe this grain should be a key ingredient. You can roast the garlic and soak the barley the day before serving. This stew with the mellow accent of roasted garlic is best made ahead. Preparation can be up to two days ahead of serving.

> 1 cup pearl barley, picked over and drained
>
> 1 head garlic (about 2 ounces)
>
> 5 tablespoons olive oil, divided
>
> 2 pounds lean, boneless beef chuck, trimmed and cut into 1-inch cubes
>
> 1 medium yellow onion, finely chopped
>
> 3 medium carrots, finely chopped
>
> 2 medium green bell peppers, finely chopped
>
> 1 quart beef stock or canned beef broth
>
> ¾ cup dry red wine
>
> 2 tablespoons tomato paste
>
> Salt and freshly ground pepper, to taste

Preheat the oven to 325F (165C). In a medium bowl, place the barley and enough warm water to cover by 3 inches. Soak for 1 hour, then drain.

Meanwhile, roast the garlic: Rub the garlic head a bit in your hands to remove some of the papery outer sheath. Slice the top ¼ inch off the garlic, exposing the tips of the individual cloves. Place the garlic in the middle of a 1-foot-long sheet of foil. Rub the bulb entirely with 1 tablespoon of the olive oil, then wrap up tightly in the foil.

Place on a pie pan or baking sheet and roast for about 1 hour or until the bulb is very soft when pierced with a fork. When cool enough to handle, break off the cloves and squeeze the cloves at the base to push the pulp out into a small bowl. Using a fork, smash into a paste and reserve until ready to use.

Heat 2 tablespoons of the oil in a medium (4- to 6-quart) cast-iron Dutch oven over medium-high heat for 1 minute. Add the beef, in batches, and sear, turning often so cubes brown evenly on all sides, 7 to 9 minutes per batch. Transfer to a medium bowl as it is browned and reserve.

Add the remaining 2 tablespoons olive oil, onion, carrots, and bell pepper to the Dutch oven and cook for 4 minutes, stirring often, until the onion is tender but not browned.

Carefully pour in the beef stock (it will splatter). Stir in the reserved beef along with the wine until well mixed and bring to a boil. Boil for 1 minute.

Reduce the heat to medium-low, and stir in the drained barley until well distributed. Simmer for 50 to 60 minutes, stirring occasionally, or until the meat is tender but not falling apart, and the barley is tender and triple its original size.

Stir in the tomato paste and reserved roasted garlic until well blended. Season to taste with salt and pepper. Transfer to a soup tureen and serve.

BEEF BROCCOLI STIR-FRY WITH GINGER

Makes 4 servings

WHEN I LIVED IN NEW York City, I made it part of my mission to taste this dish at as many Chinese-American restaurants as possible. Those restaurant chefs had the distinct advantage over the home cook, because they were able to use very high heat under their woks, not to mention the fact that their woks were not made of the flimsy metal that mine at home was. That's why I was ecstatic when I received a cast-iron wok from the Lodge Manufacturing Company of Tennessee, because I could finally do this dish justice. The first thing I did was reach for a recipe from my book *The Instant Ethnic Cook,* which I modified with the following result.

2 tablespoons cornstarch

¼ cup cold water

3 tablespoons peanut oil

3 cloves garlic, crushed through a garlic press

2 1-inch pieces fresh ginger, peeled and minced

1-pound piece boneless beef tenderloin, trimmed, cut in half lengthwise, then cut crosswise into ⅛-inch-thick slices

1 cup canned beef broth

2 tablespoons soy sauce

1½ pounds broccoli, cut into small florets

Hot cooked rice, to serve

Stir the cornstarch and cold water together in a small bowl until the cornstarch is completely dissolved and the mixture is blended and smooth. Set aside until ready to use.

Add the oil to a cast-iron wok, rotating the wok to coat the sides, and heat over high heat until the oil is rippling, about 1 minute.

Add the garlic and ginger and stir-fry (caution: the oil will splatter) until mixture is aromatic but not browned, about 1 second. Add the beef and stir-fry until the beef loses its redness and just turns brown (but only partially cooked), 2 to 3 minutes. Using a slotted spoon, transfer the beef to a plate and reserve.

Working quickly, add the beef broth and soy sauce to the wok and bring to a boil. Add the broccoli and cook for 2 minutes, stirring constantly. Reduce the heat to low, cover with foil, and simmer, stirring once, until the broccoli is crisp-tender, 1 to 2 minutes.

Increase the heat to high and add the reserved beef to the wok. Stir the reserved cornstarch mixture to recombine. Then gradually stir the cornstarch mixture into the wok. Cook, stirring constantly, until the sauce thickens and coats the stir-fry mixture with a glossy coating and the beef is fully cooked and tender, about 1 minute.

Remove the wok from the heat and transfer the stir-fry to a heated serving platter. Pour the sauce over the meat and vegetables, and serve at once over the hot cooked rice.

BEEF POT PIE IN A SKILLET

Makes 4 servings

USE A 10-INCH CAST-IRON SKILLET (nothing smaller or larger) for this voluptuous homemade pot pie. It's meat and potatoes under an oregano-infused crust—a great way to use leftover cooked beef and boiling potatoes.

CRUST

> 2½ cups all-purpose flour
>
> 1 teaspoon salt
>
> 1 tablespoon dried oregano
>
> 1 stick (½ cup) unsalted butter, cut into ¼-inch-cubes, chilled
>
> 1 large egg yolk beaten with 2 tablespoons water
>
> 1 to 5 tablespoons ice water

FILLING

> 4 tablespoons (½ stick) unsalted butter
>
> 2 medium yellow onions, finely chopped
>
> 3 carrots, cut into ⅛-inch-thick slices
>
> ¼ cup all-purpose flour
>
> 3 beef bouillon cubes dissolved in ½ cup boiling water
>
> ½ cup dry red wine
>
> 2 teaspoons dried oregano
>
> 1 teaspoon salt
>
> ½ teaspoon freshly ground pepper
>
> 3 ribs celery, finely chopped
>
> 8 ounces white button mushrooms, stemmed and thinly sliced
>
> 1 cup thawed frozen or fresh green peas
>
> 2½ pounds boneless beef, cooked (6 cups ½-inch cubed cooked beef)
>
> 2 cups diced cooked boiling potatoes

GLAZE

> 1 large egg yolk beaten with 1 tablespoon heavy cream

TO MAKE THE CRUST: Stir together the flour, salt, and oregano until well blended. Using a pastry blender or fork, cut in the chilled butter until the mixture resembles coarse cornmeal. Stir in the egg yolk beaten with water until well blended. Then add the ice water, 1 tablespoon at a time, as needed to allow the dough to form but not become sticky. Shape into a flat disk. Wrap in waxed paper, then plastic wrap, and chill at least 30 minutes or until ready to use.

Preheat the oven to 375F (190C). To prepare the filling: Melt the butter in a medium (10- to 12-inch) cast-iron skillet over medium heat. Raise the heat to medium-high and cook the onions and carrots, stirring often, until the carrots are soft but not browned, 6 to 10 minutes.

Stir in the flour until well blended and cook, stirring constantly, for 1 minute. Remove the skillet from the heat.

Stir in the dissolved bouillon, wine, oregano, salt, and pepper until well blended. Stir in the celery, mushrooms, and peas until well distributed. Stir in the beef and potatoes until well distributed.

On a lightly floured work surface, roll out the dough into a ½-inch-thick round. Trim the edges of the circle to fit the top of the skillet with a 1-inch overhang. Place the round gently on top of the skillet and pinch the dough to seal it to the skillet edge. Either cut a steam vent with a cookie cutter or make two diagonal slashes in the crust to expose the filling. Brush crust lightly with egg glaze. Place the skillet on a baking sheet and let stand for 10 minutes before baking.

Bake the pie for 35 to 40 minutes or until crust is golden brown. Let stand for 5 minutes and serve directly from the skillet.

BOEUF À LA BOURGUIGNONNE

THE TRANSLATION OF THIS FAMOUS dish is "beef stewed in the Burgundy style." I have kept it in its classic form, complete with the flourish of garnishes. This is the kind of one-dish meal that you want to cozy up to for a Sunday dinner, especially after its simmering fills your kitchen with its intoxicating scent. Words cannot do it justice. You'll just have to experience for yourself how meltingly tender and sublime the beef becomes, and how the full, rich flavor of the vegetables are called forth when cooked in this manner.

MARINADE

3 cups red Burgundy wine

½ cup brandy

1 large onion, thinly sliced

Bouquet garni (see below)

1 teaspoon salt

STEW

3 pounds boneless beef, preferably chuck, cut into 1½-inch cubes

8 strips bacon, julienned (Stack the strips and cut the stack crosswise into ¼-inch-wide pieces.)

4 tablespoons (½ stick) unsalted butter

2 medium onions, finely chopped

3 carrots, finely chopped

1 heaping tablespoon all-purpose flour

2 to 4 cups canned beef broth

Bouquet garni (see below)

3 cloves garlic, crushed through a garlic press

½ teaspoon salt

½ teaspoon freshly ground black pepper

GARNISH

1½ pounds white pearl onions, peeled (see below)

¼ cup sugar

1 stick (½ cup) unsalted butter, divided

Salt and freshly ground pepper, to taste

¾ pound white button mushrooms, stems removed and caps left whole

1 tablespoon olive oil

6 slices white bread, crusts removed, cut into triangles

½ cup finely chopped fresh parsley

TO MAKE THE MARINADE: Combine all the ingredients for the marinade in a large glass or stainless-steel bowl and stir in the beef until well combined. Cover and refrigerate for at least 6 hours and preferably overnight.

TO MAKE THE STEW: Remove the beef from the marinade. Strain the marinade, discard any solids left behind (including the bouquet garni), and reserve the marinade at room temperature until ready to use. Drain the beef, pat dry with paper towels, and reserve separately from the marinade until ready to use.

Add the bacon to a medium (4- to 6-quart) cast-iron Dutch oven and place over medium heat. Fry the bacon until crisp, about 6 minutes. Remove the bacon with a slotted spoon and reserve, leaving the drippings in the Dutch oven.

Set the Dutch oven over medium-high heat, add the butter, and heat until melted. Raise the heat to high, and add the beef in batches of a single layer. Brown, turning the pieces often so they brown evenly, 7 to 9 minutes per batch. Transfer the beef to a bowl as it is browned.

Add the onions, then the carrots, in batches, and cook until lightly browned, 4 to 5 minutes per batch. Add them to the bowl and reserve until ready to use.

Whisk the flour into the juices in the Dutch oven and place over medium-high heat. Stir in the reserved marinade and cook, whisking constantly across the bottom of the skillet and along the sides, until the sauce is smooth, about 4 minutes.

Add the reserved beef, bacon, onions, and carrots with any drippings to the Dutch oven. Add enough broth to cover the contents by 2 inches. Place the Dutch oven over medium-high heat and bring to a boil.

Stir in the bouquet garni, garlic, salt, and pepper. Reduce the heat to medium-low, cover, and simmer, stirring occasionally, until the beef is very tender but not falling apart, 2 to 3 hours. Remove and discard the bouquet garni.

MEANWHILE, PREPARE THE GARNISH: Place the pearl onions in a large (12- to 14-inch) cast-iron skillet and set over medium-high heat. Stir in the sugar, 2 tablespoons of the butter, a little salt and pepper, and enough water to cover by ¼ inch. Bring to a boil. Raise the heat to high and boil vigorously until the water is reduced to a ⅛ cup (it should be a syrupy brown glaze) and the onions are tender, about 20 to 25 minutes, shaking the skillet occasionally so that the onions are coated and become a light golden brown. Be careful not to burn the onions. Stir the onions frequently during the last 5 to 10 minutes.

Meanwhile, in a medium (10- to 12-inch) cast-iron skillet, melt 2 tablespoons of the butter over medium heat, add the mushrooms, and cook, stirring often, until the mushrooms are browned, about 8 minutes.

In large (12- to 14-inch) cast-iron skillet over medium heat, melt the remaining 4 tablespoons butter. Stir in the oil and fry the bread until a light golden brown, about 2 minutes on each side. Keep the garnishes warm until ready to use.

Using a slotted spoon, transfer the beef to a large oval gratin dish. Distribute the garnishes over and around the meat.

Meanwhile, raise the heat under the Dutch oven to high and bring to a boil. Boil the remaining contents for about 10 minutes or until reduced by about ¼. The flavor should be very rich and concentrated; reduce more if necessary. Pour some of the sauce over the beef, sprinkle with parsley, and serve the remaining sauce separately in a sauceboat. Serve at once.

T IP: **BOUQUET GARNI**

To make a *bouquet garni*: Place 2 sprigs each fresh parsley, thyme, and rosemary, 2 bay leaves, and 12 whole black peppercorns in a 5-inch-square piece of clean, new cheesecloth. Gather and tie the bundle tightly with string. This allows for the easy removal of these herbs and spices before the dish is served.

T ECHNIQUE: **TO PEEL PEARL ONIONS**

Parboil the onions in boiling water for 1 minute. Drain in a colander under cold running water. Trim off and discard the root base of each onion and then pinch the stem end; by doing this the onion will slip easily out of its papery sheath.

Slow-Roasted Barbecue Brisket

Makes 4 to 6 servings

I KNOW WE LIVE IN an era where we are crunched for time, but I also know that we all secretly (some of us not so secretly) crave slow-roasted food. And roasting is one of the many culinary techniques in which cast-iron cookware excels over other cookware.

Please be careful when handling the cayenne and chili powder for the dry rub. Do not touch your face or eyes, because the cayenne and chili powder can act as irritants.

DRY RUB

¼ cup firmly packed light-brown sugar

1 teaspoon garlic powder

1 teaspoon chili powder

1 teaspoon salt

1 teaspoon freshly ground pepper

1 teaspoon paprika

¼ teaspoon ground cayenne pepper

BRISKET

1 (4-pound) boneless beef brisket

2 tablespoons olive oil

Preheat the oven to 300F (150C). To make the dry rub: Combine all the dry rub ingredients in a small bowl and stir until well combined.

TO PREPARE THE BRISKET: Rub the dry rub into all the sides of the brisket. Spread the oil over the bottom of a medium (6- to 8-quart) cast-iron Dutch oven.

Place the brisket in the oiled Dutch oven and bake, covered, in the lower third of the oven for 2 hours, turning the meat every half hour. (Note: If there is not enough liquid to prevent the brisket from burning, add up to 2 cups warm water around, not over or on the brisket, so as not to disturb the dry rub.)

Increase the heat to 350F (175C). Bake the brisket, covered, for 1 to 1½ hours more or until it is very tender but not falling apart; however, you should almost be able to slice it with a fork. (Note: If there is not enough liquid to prevent the brisket from burning, add up to ½ cup warm water around, not over or on the brisket, so as not to disturb the dry rub.)

To serve, cut the brisket diagonally across the grain into ¼-inch-thick slices and serve drizzled with the cooking liquid from the Dutch oven.

CAESAR SALAD BURGERS

THIS IS CAESAR SALAD METAMORPHOSED into a burger with the same elements (and then some). For example, the bread loaves that cradle the burgers are in place of the croutons of the classic salad. And a cast-iron skillet makes an amazingly yummy burger—some say better than a grill does. I find that a premium bottled Caesar salad dressing (available from supermarkets) works well for this recipe. If you can't find the small loaves, simply cut a larger loaf into 5-inch-long pieces.

> 4 (5- to 7-inch-long) Italian or French breads, to serve
>
> ½ head Romaine lettuce, shredded (10 to 12 ounces total)
>
> 1 medium tomato, cut into 4 slices

BURGERS
> 1 pound ground beef
>
> 2 tablespoons ketchup
>
> 1 teaspoon Dijon mustard
>
> ¼ cup capers, drained
>
> 3 tablespoons minced fresh basil
>
> ½ teaspoon salt
>
> ¼ teaspoon freshly ground pepper
>
> 1 tablespoon olive oil

TOPPING
> ¼ cup freshly grated Parmesan cheese
>
> Homemade or store-bought bottled Caesar salad dressing

Slit open each bread loaf lengthwise and place a loaf on each of 4 plates. Top the bottom half with the lettuce and tomato and reserve until ready to serve.

TO PREPARE THE BURGERS: In a medium bowl, gently stir together all the burger ingredients except the oil until well blended.

Using your hands, shape the burger mixture into 4 flat ¾-inch-thick patties. Place a large (12- to 14-inch) cast-iron skillet over medium heat. Add the oil and heat for 2 minutes. Add the burgers and cook in a single layer (not overlapping) for 4 to 5 minutes on each side for medium-rare, 5 to 6 minutes on each side for well-done.

To serve, working quickly, place a burger on the bottom half of each reserved bread loaf and sprinkle with the Parmesan cheese. Drizzle with some dressing, lean the bread loaf top against the bread loaf bottom, and serve at once.

CHICKEN-FRIED STEAK

SOME SOUTHERNERS AND MIDWESTERNERS CALL this dish "smothered steak" or "country-fried steak." This recipe is a great excuse to savor bacon one morning so you will have the drippings to make this dish. The country gravy that accompanies it should be so liberally seasoned to taste with freshly ground black pepper that the gravy looks "dusty." I first tasted this dish in Oklahoma City, and it was *sooooo* good I immediately ordered a plate to go—before I even finished my lunch of it. I flavored my version of this stick-to-your-ribs meal with some onion and cayenne.

1 large egg, beaten

1¼ cups milk, at room temperature

1 cup unseasoned dry bread crumbs

¼ teaspoon ground cayenne pepper

½ teaspoon salt

4 beef cube steaks (1 pound total)

¼ cup plus 2 tablespoons bacon drippings

1 cup minced yellow onion

1 tablespoon all-purpose flour

1 cup heavy cream, at room temperature

Salt and freshly ground pepper, to taste

2 tablespoons minced fresh parsley

Preheat the oven to 200F (95C). In a medium bowl, combine the egg and ¼ cup of the milk and whisk until well blended. In another medium bowl, combine the bread crumbs, cayenne, and salt and stir with a fork until well blended. Transfer the crumb mixture to a large plate.

One at a time, dip each steak into the egg mixture, letting the excess drain back into the bowl. Then coat the steak with the crumb mixture on both sides. Transfer the coated steaks to a piece of waxed paper.

Heat the ¼ cup bacon drippings in a large (12- to 14-inch) cast-iron skillet over medium-high heat for 2 minutes. Add the steaks and cook until cooked throughout and golden brown, 2 to 3 minutes on each side. Transfer the steaks to a baking sheet and hold in the warm oven while making the gravy.

Meanwhile, add the 2 tablespoons bacon drippings to the skillet with its juices and set over medium heat. Add the onion and cook, scraping up any browned bits from the bottom of the skillet, until the onion is translucent, about 1 minute. Sprinkle the onion with the flour and cook, stirring, for 30 seconds.

Gradually whisk in the cream and remaining 1 cup milk and bring to a boil. Cook, whisking occasionally, until thickened, 5 to 8 minutes. Season the gravy generously with salt and pepper and stir in the parsley until well blended. Top the steaks with gravy and serve at once.

CHILI CON CARNE WITH TOPPINGS

THE ART OF MAKING A great chili is in the balance of ingredients. Therefore, I cannot emphasize enough the importance of tasting this dish during cooking and again at the end of cooking time and adjusting the seasonings accordingly. If you grind your own chili powder, even better, but if it's very strong, then use less than I call for because my recipe is based on the more widely used, and much milder, prepared brands.

2 tablespoons vegetable oil

2⅔ pounds lean boneless beef, preferably round steak, cut into 1-inch cubes

2 pounds fresh Mexican chorizo or spicy Spanish smoked pork-based sausages, removed from their casings and coarsely chopped

3 medium yellow onions, coarsely chopped

5 cloves garlic, crushed through a garlic press

2 fresh jalapeño chiles, seeded, ribs removed, and minced

1 (4-ounce) can chopped mild green chiles, drained

3 to 4 tablespoons chili powder, depending on strength

2 teaspoons ground cumin

1 tablespoon dried oregano, preferably Mexican (available from Mexican markets)

2 (28-ounce cans) whole tomatoes

1 (12-ounce) bottle dark ale or beer, preferably Mexican

½ cup tequila

1 cup canned beef broth

3 tablespooons unsweetened cocoa powder

½ teaspoon ground cinnamon

Salt and freshly ground pepper, to taste

Light brown sugar, to taste

TOPPINGS (OPTIONAL)

½ cup finely chopped fresh cilantro

1 (15-ounce) can red kidney beans, drained

Shredded sharp cheddar cheese

Thinly sliced scallions

COOKING IN CAST IRON

Sliced, pitted black olives

Sour cream, to serve

Heat the oil in a large (6- to 8-quart) cast-iron Dutch oven over medium-high heat for 1 minute. Add the beef and cook, turning the beef often so it browns on all sides, 7 to 9 minutes. Using a slotted spoon, transfer to a bowl and reserve.

Add the chorizo to the Dutch oven and cook, stirring constantly, until browned, 8 minutes. Using a slotted spoon, transfer the chorizo to the bowl with the beef and reserve until ready to use.

Add the onion and garlic to the Dutch oven and cook, stirring, for 1 minute. Add the reserved meats, jalapeño chiles, green chiles, chili powder, cumin, and oregano and mix until combined. Stir in the tomatoes, ale, tequila, beef broth, cocoa powder, and cinnamon until well blended. Bring to a boil.

Reduce the heat to medium-low and simmer, stirring often, for 2 hours. Season with salt, pepper, and brown sugar. Serve hot, passing the toppings separately, if desired.

PASTA WITH HOT ITALIAN SAUSAGE AND POTATOES

Makes 4 servings

THIS DISH COULD EASILY FEED six diners; simply increase the amount of pasta to 1½ pounds total.

> 1 pound boiling potatoes, cut into ½-inch cubes
>
> 2 tablespoons olive oil
>
> 2 pounds fresh sweet or hot bulk Italian sausage
>
> 2 medium white onions, thinly sliced
>
> 2 green bell peppers, cut in half lengthwise and thinly sliced
>
> 2 (14½-ounce) cans stewed tomatoes
>
> 1 cup dry red wine
>
> ¼ cup balsamic vinegar
>
> 3 tablespoons fennel seeds (available from supermarkets)
>
> 1 tablespoon sugar
>
> Salt and freshly ground pepper, to taste
>
> 1 pound rigatoni pasta
>
> Freshly grated Parmesan cheese, to serve

In a saucepan of boiling water, boil the potatoes until tender yet still firm, 12 to 13 minutes. Drain the potatoes and reserve until ready to use.

Heat 1 tablespoon of the oil in a medium (4- to 6-quart) cast-iron Dutch oven over medium-high heat for 1 minute. Add the sausage and cook until golden brown all over, breaking up the bulk sausage with a fork, 6 to 8 minutes. Transfer to a bowl until ready to use.

Carefully pour off the grease from the Dutch oven and return to medium-high heat. Add the remaining 1 tablespoon oil. Add the onions and cook until lightly golden brown, 3 minutes. Stir in the bell peppers and cook for 1 minute. Transfer the vegetables to the bowl with the sausage.

Place the Dutch oven over medium-low heat. Stir in the tomatoes, wine, balsamic vinegar, fennel seeds, and sugar. Cook, partially covered, for 35 minutes, stirring occasionally. Stir in the reserved potatoes. Season with salt and pepper.

Meanwhile, about 10 minutes before serving, bring 3 quarts of water to boil in a 6- to 8-quart pot over high heat. Stir in the pasta and bring back to the boil. Boil until al dente (slightly firm to the bite), 7 to 9 minutes, stirring occasionally, and drain.

To serve, divide the pasta among dinner plates, ladle the sausage mixture over the top, sprinkle with Parmesan cheese, and serve hot.

MIDWESTERN CHEESE-STUFFED MEAT LOAF

Makes 4 to 6 servings

YOU SHOULD HAVE SEEN MY glee when I first tasted this recipe. Stuffed meat loaf has ruined me for any other meat loaf. Now when I am served meat loaf (one of my favorite comfort foods), I find I am disappointed if it doesn't envelop some wonderful ingredient, like the soothing, creamy, oozy, mozzarella cheese you'll encounter with this recipe.

1 pound ground beef

½ pound ground veal

¼ pound ground pork

1 teaspoon salt

1 teaspoon freshly ground pepper

2 tablespoons chili powder

⅔ cup unseasoned dry bread crumbs

1 large egg, lightly beaten

¼ cup milk

1 medium yellow onion, minced

3 cloves garlic, crushed through a garlic press

1 (4-ounce) jar pimientos, drained

1 teaspoon olive oil

11 ounces sliced mozzarella cheese

1 tablespoon all-purpose flour

Preheat the oven to 350F (175C). Combine the beef, veal, pork, salt, pepper, chili powder, and bread crumbs in a large bowl. Stir in the egg, milk, onion, garlic, and pimientos until the mixture is thoroughly blended.

Lightly brush a 15-inch-long sheet of foil with the oil. Wet your hands and turn the meat mixture out onto the foil and shape into a firm, 1-inch-thick, 14 × 8-inch rectangle.

Layer 6 ounces of the cheese slices over the rectangle, leaving a 2-inch border uncovered around the edges. Lifting the foil up as an aid and starting with the short end, roll the meat up tightly, jelly-roll style.

When you've formed the roll, wet your hands again and completely seal in the filling by crimping the ends and seam.

Transfer the meat loaf, seam side down, to a 9 × 5-inch cast-iron loaf pan, discarding the foil used for rolling. Sprinkle the top of the meat loaf evenly with the flour.

Bake on the middle oven rack for 1 to 1¼ hours, or until the meat loaf starts to shrink away from the sides of the pan and the top is well browned.

Remove the pan from the oven and carefully pour off the excess fat surrounding the meat loaf.

Top the loaf with the remaining 5 ounces cheese slices, then return to the oven for 5 minutes or until the cheese melts. To serve, let stand for 10 minutes before slicing.

PAN-SEARED STEAKS WITH SHIITAKE MUSHROOMS

INDULGE YOURSELF WITH A STEAK dinner that delivers. Thirty minutes before you plan to cook these steaks, remove them from the refrigerator so they can come to room temperature to ensure that they cook evenly. Another must for an impeccably cooked steak is to never pierce the meat, which allows all the precious juices to run out. Rather, use a pair of wooden tongs. (You can purchase these at a kitchenware shop.) An added benefit: The wood won't scratch the cast-iron skillet, whereas metal will.

4 (6- to 8-ounce) boneless strip steaks (prime or choice)

¾ teaspoon freshly ground black pepper

4 tablespoons (½ stick) unsalted butter

1 medium white onion, coarsely chopped

8 ounces shiitake or cremini mushrooms, stemmed and thinly sliced

Place the steaks on a sheet of waxed paper and evenly coat both sides with the black pepper and reserve at room temperature (up to 30 minutes) until ready to use.

Place a large (12- to 14-inch) cast-iron skillet over medium-high heat and allow it to heat for about 1½ minutes or until a drop of water dances on its surface.

Working quickly, add the butter, onion, and mushrooms to the skillet. Cook until the onions are tender and the mushrooms have released most of their moisture, stirring often, about 5 minutes. Transfer the mixture to a heatproof platter and place in a warm oven.

Place the skillet over medium-high heat and heat for 2 minutes or until a drop of water vaporizes instantly on its surface.

Add the steaks to the skillet and cook until they are seared long enough that they can be loosened to turn, 1½ to 2 minutes. Reduce the heat to medium, flip the steaks over, and cook for 2 minutes for rare. Cook longer for increased doneness.

Working quickly, remove the warm serving platter with the mushroom mixture and add the steaks, spooning some of the juices over the steaks. Serve at once.

VITELLO TONNATO

Makes 4 servings

I FIRST CREATED A VERSION of this traditional Italian recipe years ago for my cookbook *Contemporary One Dish Meals*. Since then, I have revisited this piquant, sophisticated meal many times. I used to pound the veal scallops, but now I omit that step in an effort to save the home cook time. The results are still fantastic. This recipe is simple when you use a premium, store-bought mayo as the base for the sauce, rather than from-scratch mayonnaise. This is an ideal meal for a summertime dinner or easy-to-serve al fresco. *Mesclun*, also called gourmet salad mix when purchased at supermarkets, is a mixture of young, small salad greens.

VEAL

1½ pounds veal scallopini (4 to 8 scallops)

Salt and freshly ground pepper

3 tablespoons unsalted butter

2 scallions, thinly sliced

2 tablespoons fresh lemon juice

SAUCE

2 cups mayonnaise

2 tablespoons fresh lemon juice, plus more if needed

½ teaspoon dry mustard

¼ cup dry white wine

2 (6-ounce) cans water-packed chunk white tuna, drained and pureed

⅓ cup minced sweet gherkin pickles

3 tablespoons capers, drained

4 flat anchovy fillets, minced

¼ teaspoon salt, plus more if needed

½ teaspoon freshly ground pepper, plus more if needed

8 ounces *mesclun* or 2 bunches watercress, to serve

2 teaspoons freshly grated lemon zest, to serve

TO PREPARE THE VEAL: Lightly season both sides of the veal scallops with salt and pepper and reserve until ready to use.

COOKING IN CAST IRON

22

Melt the butter in a large (12- to 14-inch) cast-iron skillet over medium heat. Add the veal and cook in batches (do not crowd the skillet, and do not overlap the veal slices) until opaque throughout, 2 to 4 minutes on each side. Transfer the veal to a serving platter. Sprinkle the veal with the scallions, drizzle with the lemon juice, and reserve at room temperature.

To make the sauce: Stir together all the sauce ingredients in a medium bowl until well blended. Adjust the seasoning with more salt, pepper, and lemon juice if needed.

To serve, arrange the mesclun around the edge of the serving platter. Ladle the tuna sauce over all, covering the surface of each veal piece, sprinkle with the lemon zest, and serve at room temperature.

VEAL CHOPS WITH MEDITERRANEAN BLACK OLIVE SAUCE

Makes 4 servings

LAST SPRING I WAS GIVEN some jars of glorious Greek kalamata olives, which inspired this dish.

> 3 tablespoons olive oil
>
> 4 (½-inch-thick) veal chops (2¼ pounds total)
>
> 1 cup canned beef broth
>
> ½ cup dry red wine
>
> ¼ cup red wine vinegar
>
> 3 cups pitted Greek kalamata olives (available from gormet shops and most supermarkets)
>
> 3 cloves garlic, crushed through a garlic press
>
> 2 teaspoons fennel seeds, lightly bruised (rolled with a rolling pin until cracked open slightly), available from supermarkets

Heat the olive oil in a large (12- to 14-inch) cast-iron skillet over medium-high heat for 2 minutes. Add the veal and sear until browned all over, 4 minutes on each side.

Meanwhile, stir together the remaining ingredients in a medium glass or stainless-steel bowl until well blended.

Transfer the veal to a baking dish (not cast iron) large enough to accommodate the veal in a single layer. Spoon the mixture around and on top of the veal, making sure it's submersed in the liquid mixture and cover.

Bake for 20 to 30 minutes, or until the veal is fork-tender. Serve the veal, topped with the sauce, at once.

SKILLET TAMALE PIE

Makes 4 to 6 servings

WHEN I BEGAN TO RESEARCH the origins of this recipe, I assumed that its roots were in the 1950s, due to the culinary aspects in America at the time. That's why, much to my surprise, after further time spent sleuthing, I turned the pages of one of my much-trusted culinary reference books, John F. Mariani's *The Dictionary of American Food and Drink*, to learn that the ". . . term first appeared in 1911"!

FILLING

2 medium yellow onions, finely chopped

2 medium green bell peppers, coarsely chopped

1 pound fresh bulk pork country sausage or fresh bulk hot Italian sausage

1 pound ground beef

¼ cup dry red wine

3 cloves garlic, crushed through a garlic press

2½ teaspoons chili powder

1 teaspoon ground cumin

2 teaspoons dried oregano

3 to 4 tablespoons minced pickled jalapeño chiles, or to taste

1 (14½-ounce) can stewed tomatoes

1 (10-ounce) package thawed, frozen corn kernels (1¾ cups)

TOPPING

2 cups canned vegetable broth

2 cups yellow cornmeal

1 teaspoon salt

1 cup cold water

1½ cups shredded sharp cheddar cheese

To prepare the filling: Place a large (12- to 14-inch) cast-iron skillet over medium heat. Add the onions and bell peppers. Cook for 3 minutes, stirring occasionally, until the bell peppers are tender.

Add the sausage, ground beef, and red wine. Cook, breaking the sausage and beef up with a fork, until they lose their pink color, 10 to 12 minutes.

Stir in the garlic, chili powder, cumin, oregano, jalapeño chiles, tomatoes, and corn until combined. Remove the skillet from the heat, and using a wooden spoon, firmly and evenly press down the contents to compact, and reserve until ready to use.

Preheat the oven to 350F (175C). Meanwhile, prepare the topping: Bring the vegetable broth to a boil in a 2- to 3-quart saucepan.

Stir the cornmeal and salt in a medium bowl until well blended. Stir in 1 cup cold water (to help prevent lumping), then stir mixture into the boiling vegetable broth.

Remove from the heat and stir the mixture until thickened, stirring briskly and constantly with a wooden spoon. (The heat from the skillet is enough to cook the mixture.) Stir the mixture until very thick and it begins to pull away from the sides of the pan, 2 to 3 minutes. It will begin to be difficult to stir. Be careful not to let it cool completely, or it will not be spreadable.

Working very quickly, spoon the cornmeal mixture over the filling in the skillet, using a knife or spatula to smooth it. The cornmeal mixture will begin to set as you work; spread evenly using a wooden spoon and your fingers if necessary.

Set the skillet on a baking sheet. Bake on the middle oven rack for 35 to 40 minutes or until heated through and the top is golden brown. Sprinkle evenly with the cheese, and bake for 5 to 10 minutes more or until the cheese is melted. Let stand 10 minutes then serve, using a slotted spoon.

JAPANESE-AMERICAN SUKIYAKI

SUKIYAKI IS KNOWN IN JAPAN as the "friendship dish" because foreigners like it. There are many regional variations, as with almost all famous dishes. Traditionally, diners dip their cooked food into raw, beaten egg; however, I have Americanized this version and omitted that step.

If you make dashi (a type of Japanese stock) or live near a health food store that sells it in instant form, use that in place of the beef broth. I love the play of textures and flavors of this dish. The mirin, dried udon noodles, and pickled ginger are available at Asian markets.

3 tablespoons peanut oil

1⅓ pounds boneless beef tenderloin, very thinly sliced across the grain

8 ounces fresh shiitake mushrooms, stemmed and very thinly sliced

5 cups canned beef broth

⅓ cup soy sauce

¼ cup mirin (Japanese rice wine)

1 pound dried udon (thick Japanese noodles) or soba noodles (Japanese buckwheat noodles)

¾ pound fresh spinach, stemmed, leaves torn into bite-sized pieces

6 ounces fresh mung bean sprouts

1 (8-ounce) can sliced water chestnuts, drained

1 (8-ounce) can sliced bamboo shoots, drained

6 scallions, thinly sliced on the diagonal

¼ cup minced pickled ginger, to serve

Add the oil to a cast-iron wok, rotating the wok to coat the sides, and heat over high heat until the oil is rippling, about 2 minutes.

Add the beef and stir-fry until the beef loses its redness and just turns brown, 2 to 3 minutes. Using a slotted spoon, transfer the beef to a plate and reserve.

Working quickly, add the mushrooms to the wok and stir-fry for 2 minutes. Add the beef broth, soy sauce, and mirin to the wok and bring to a boil.

Add the noodles and stir to combine. Reduce the heat to medium-high and return to the boil. Boil until al dente (slightly firm to the bite), stirring occasionally, 6 to 10 minutes. Stir in the spinach, bean sprouts, water chestnuts, bamboo shoots, and scallions to the wok, and stir until well distributed and just until heated throughout, about 30 seconds.

Just before serving, stir in the reserved beef. Serve in soup bowls, sprinkle with the pickled ginger, and serve at once.

POLISH STUFFED CABBAGE LEAVES

Makes 4 servings (3 stuffed cabbage rolls each)

A MORE CONTEMPORARY VERSION OF stuffed cabbage, the cabbage filling is accented with walnuts, currants, and dill. The brothlike sauce contains brandy and mushrooms. Dried zante currants are available in supermarkets, or health food stores. I have tried using raisins in place of currants for this dish but they throw the flavor balance off.

1 (3-pound) head green cabbage

FILLING

½ pound ground beef

¼ pound ground pork

1 cup cooked white rice, at room temperature

1 cup minced white onion

2 scallions, green part only, thinly sliced

⅔ cup coarsely chopped walnuts

½ cup dried zante currants (available at supermarkets or health food stores)

2 teaspoons minced fresh dill

½ teaspoon salt

¼ teaspoon ground pepper

⅓ teaspoon ground nutmeg

1 large egg, slightly beaten

SAUCE

3 cups canned beef broth

12 ounces white button mushrooms, stemmed and thinly sliced

½ cup brandy

1 (28-ounce) can diced tomatoes

⅓ cup heavy cream, at room temperature

Salt and freshly ground pepper, to taste

Core the cabbage and carefully peel off the 12 largest leaves and set them aside. Chop enough of the remaining cabbage to make 2 cups of finely chopped cabbage and reserve.

Boil the leaves in water to cover just until limp and tender, about 3 minutes. Rinse in a colander under cold, running water. Drain well and set aside.

Make the filling: In a medium bowl, stir together the beef, pork, reserved 2 cups chopped cabbage, rice, onion, scallions, walnuts, currants, dill, salt, pepper, nutmeg, and egg until well blended.

Spread the leaves out, cupped side up, on a work surface with the stem ends facing you.

Preheat the oven to 375F (190C). Shape a firmly packed ⅓ cup filling into a 2½-inch-long log. Place filling 1 inch above the stem end of a leaf. Fold the stem end of the leaf over the filling. While rolling the leaf upward, fold the sides of the leaf inward and over the filling, rolling the leaf tightly to enclose the filling. Repeat with the remaining cabbage leaves and filling.

Pour the beef broth into a medium (4- to 6-quart) cast-iron Dutch oven. Place the cabbage rolls, seam side down, into the Dutch oven in a single layer so that the rolls are covered by the broth.

Bake, covered, for 1 hour, or until cooked through. Transfer the rolls to a serving dish and keep warm until ready to serve.

Meanwhile, prepare the sauce: Transfer the cooking liquid in the Dutch oven to a 2- to 3-quart saucepan along with the mushrooms and place over medium heat. Cook, stirring, until the mushrooms are tender, 10 minutes. Stir in the brandy, tomatoes, and heavy cream until well blended, and cook, stirring, for 1 minute more. Season with salt and pepper. Ladle the sauce over the cabbage rolls, and serve in shallow soup bowls.

SLOPPY JOES WITH TRI-COLORED BELL PEPPERS

Makes 4 servings

THIS RECIPE IS BEST MADE the day ahead, to allow the flavors to marry. I like to use a flavorful ground beef with more fat and simply drain off the fat after cooking as instructed in the following recipe.

1 tablespoon vegetable oil

1 medium yellow onion, finely chopped

3 cloves garlic, crushed through a garlic press

1 small green bell pepper, finely diced

1 small red bell pepper, finely diced

1 small yellow bell pepper, finely diced

1¼ pounds ground beef

½ cup molasses

1 (14½-ounce) can stewed tomatoes

3 tablespoons tomato paste

3 tablespoons distilled white vinegar

2 tablespoons chili powder

1 teaspoon ground allspice

¼ teaspoon ground cloves

3 scallions, including green parts, thinly sliced

Salt and freshly ground pepper, to taste

4 split hamburger buns, toasted, to serve

Heat the oil in a large (12- to 14-inch) cast-iron skillet over medium heat for 1 minute. Add the onion and cook, stirring often, until soft but not browned, 3 to 4 minutes. Stir in the garlic and bell peppers and cook, stirring, until the peppers are tender, 5 minutes.

Add the ground beef and cook, using a wooden spoon to break up the clumps of beef, just until the beef begins to brown, 5 minutes. Carefully drain off any fat.

Stir in the molasses, tomatoes, tomato paste, and vinegar until well blended and bring to a boil. Reduce the heat to low and stir in the chili powder, allspice, and cloves.

Simmer, stirring occasionally, until slightly thickened, 10 to 15 minutes. (Note: The mixture will have a fair amount of liquid.) Stir in the scallions and season to taste with salt and pepper.

Arrange each toasted bun on a dinner plate, ladle some of the Sloppy Joe mixture over the bottom half of each bun, and lean the top against it, serving open faced.

SAUERBRATEN

THIS GERMAN SPECIALTY OF TENDER beef partnered with a gingersnap-infused sauce is punctuated with golden raisins. Though many of us are not used to the idea of such a sauce with beef, it is more common in other areas of the world. For a side, serve small boiled potatoes with a pat of butter and a sprinkling of parsley. I have incorporated many shortcuts in this recipe, among them the use of a prepared pickling spice available in supermarkets. I like McCormick's mixture of cinnamon bark, whole allspice, mustard seed, coriander seeds, bay leaves, ginger, chiles, cloves, black pepper, mace, and cardamom.

MEAT

> 2 tablespoons olive oil
>
> 1 (2-pound) boneless beef brisket
>
> 1 cup dry red wine
>
> ¼ cup red wine vinegar
>
> 1 cup canned beef broth
>
> 1 large white onion, thinly sliced
>
> ⅛ cup firmly packed dark brown sugar
>
> 2 tablespoons mixed pickling spice or 1 teaspoon whole black peppercorns, 1 teaspoon yellow mustard seeds, 8 juniper berries, lightly bruised (rolled with a rolling pin until cracked open slightly), 4 whole cloves, and 1 bay leaf

SAUCE

> ½ cup sour cream, at room temperature
>
> ½ cup golden raisins (available at supermarkets and health food stores)
>
> 1 cup finely crushed gingersnap cookies (about 14)
>
> Salt and freshly ground pepper, to taste

TO PREPARE THE MEAT: Heat the oil in a medium (4- to 6-quart) cast-iron Dutch oven over medium-high heat for 2 minutes. Add the brisket and sear until browned evenly, about 4 minutes on each side.

Add the remaining meat ingredients and bring to a boil.

Meanwhile, preheat the oven to 325F (165C).

Cover the Dutch oven and transfer to the oven, placing in the lower third of the oven. Bake for 2 to 2½ hours or until fork-tender but not falling apart, turning the brisket over every 30 minutes and replacing the lid.

Using a slotted spoon, remove the meat from the Dutch oven. Slice thinly, arranging the slices on a warmed serving platter. Cover and keep warm until ready to serve.

MEANWHILE, TO PREPARE THE SAUCE: Strain the cooking liquid remaining in the Dutch oven, discarding any solids, and transfer the liquid to a 1- to 2-quart saucepan (not cast iron) and set over low heat. In a small bowl, stir ¼ cup of the hot cooking liquid into the sour cream and stir this mixture back into the saucepan. Cook gently, stirring constantly, for 3 minutes. Do not allow to boil.

Stir in the raisins and crushed gingersnaps and cook gently, stirring constantly, for 2 minutes more or until the gingersnaps have dissolved and the sauce has thickened. (If the sauce is too thick, stir in up to 1 cup of hot water until well blended.) Season with salt and pepper, ladle the sauce over the warm meat, and serve at once.

SALTIMBOCCA

THE ROMAN DISH SALTIMBOCCA MEANS "jump mouth" in Italian. The flavors of this outstanding dish do just that—jump in your mouth. From beginning to end, the medium cast-iron skillet does a magnificent job of cooking the dish so that the integrity of each element stays intact. When purchasing the veal and prosciutto, buy 8 pieces each so you have 2 each per sandwich. Prosciutto is a salt-cured, seasoned (but not smoked) Italian ham. Italy's prosciutto from Parma is the true prosciutto, though there are others now made in the United States. Prosciutto is available in gourmet and Italian markets and many supermarkets.

VEAL

8 (about 3-ounce) veal scallops (about 1½ pounds total)

⅓ pound prosciutto, cut into 8 slices

½ cup freshly grated Parmesan cheese

2 tablespoons minced fresh sage leaves

2 large eggs

1½ cups all-purpose flour

1 teaspoon salt

4 tablespoons (½ stick) unsalted butter

SAUCE

1 cup Marsala (an Italian fortified wine)

1 cup canned beef broth

1 stick (½ cup) unsalted butter

Salt and freshly ground pepper, to taste

TO PREPARE THE VEAL: On a baking sheet covered with waxed paper, lay the 4 largest scallops flat and place 2 slices of prosciutto on each. Fold over the prosciutto so that as little of the prosciutto hangs over the veal as possible.

Divide the Parmesan cheese and sage evenly among the 4 scallops, sprinkling an even layer on top of the prosciutto. Top with the remaining 4 scallops, like a sandwich. Using your fingers, press these layers lightly to remove any air pockets. Cover with more waxed paper and refrigerate for 10 minutes.

Beat the eggs in a medium bowl until lemon colored. Using a fork, stir together the flour and salt in another medium bowl.

Carefully dip each veal "sandwich" (so as not to disturb the filling) first into the egg, then into the flour mixture to coat it evenly, gently shaking off any excess flour.

Preheat the oven to 325F (165C). Heat 2 tablespoons of the butter in a medium (10- to 12-inch) cast-iron skillet over medium heat until melted. Add the veal and cook until browned on the bottom, 6 minutes. Add the remaining 2 tablespoons butter to the skillet and carefully flip the veal over (so as not to disturb the filling) and cook until browned, another 6 minutes.

Transfer the skillet to the oven and cook for 15 to 20 minutes or until no more pink remains in the veal (the prosciutto will remain pink). Cover to keep warm until ready to serve.

MEANWHILE, TO MAKE THE SAUCE: Add the Marsala and beef broth to a heavy 3- to 4-quart saucepan and place over medium-high heat. Boil until the liquid is reduced to ½ cup, 7 to 10 minutes.

Reduce the heat to medium and add the ½ cup butter, whisking until the butter is melted and the sauce well blended. Remove the saucepan from the heat and season to taste with salt and pepper. Spoon the sauce around the Saltimbocca and serve at once.

BEEF STROGANOFF

THIS DISH IS A CLASSIC hallmark, to which I have added some woodsy cremini mushrooms. Cremini are a less-mature form of portobello mushrooms and are available in many supermarkets today.

2 tablespoons plus 2 teaspoons olive oil

1½ pounds boneless beef sirloin steak, cut crosswise into thin strips

2 medium yellow onions, finely chopped

8 ounces white button mushrooms, stemmed and thinly sliced

8 ounces cremini or portobello mushrooms, stemmed and thinly sliced

1 pound dry extra-wide egg noodles

3 tablespoons unsalted butter

3 tablespoons all-purpose flour

2 tablespoons tomato paste

1½ cups canned beef broth

½ cup dry white wine

1 cup sour cream, at room temperature

Salt and freshly ground pepper, to taste

Heat the 2 tablespoons oil in a large (12- to 14-inch) cast-iron skillet over medium heat for 2 minutes. Stir in the steak and cook, stirring often, until browned all over and cooked throughout, 5 to 8 minutes. Transfer the steak to a bowl and reserve until ready to use.

Return the skillet with the cooking juices to the heat and add the 2 teaspoons oil. Add the onions and mushrooms. Cook the mixture, stirring frequently, until the mushrooms are wilted and a light golden brown, 7 to 9 minutes, then transfer to the bowl with the steak.

Meanwhile, bring 3 quarts of water to a boil in a 6- to 8-quart pot over medium heat. Stir in the noodles and return to the boil. Boil, stirring the noodles occasionally, until al dente (slightly firm to the bite), 6 to 8 minutes.

While the noodles are cooking, place the skillet with its juices over medium-low heat and melt the butter. Whisk in the flour and cook for 2 minutes, whisking constantly. Do not allow to brown.

Whisk in the tomato paste, beef broth, and wine until well blended. Raise the heat to medium and bring to a boil. Cook, whisking constantly, until thickened, 4 to 5 minutes.

Stir in the reserved steak mixture and cook, stirring, until heated through, 1 minute.

Remove the skillet from the heat, and transfer to a serving dish. Gradually stir in the sour cream until well blended, and season with salt and pepper.

Drain the noodles well and divide among 4 heated plates. Spoon a portion of the stroganoff over each serving and serve at once.

MOUTHWATERING YANKEE POT ROAST

ONE OF THE MANY QUALITY convenience products available in the supermarkets now is "ready-to-eat" (already washed, peeled, and trimmed) baby carrots. They save time, are tender and tasty, and make for a pretty presentation, as illustrated by this national dish.

3 cups canned beef broth, plus 3 cups more, if necessary

2 cups dry red wine

1 (28-ounce) can diced tomatoes

10 whole cloves

1 (3½-pound) boneless beef chuck roast

½ teaspoon salt

1 teaspoon freshly ground pepper

½ cup all-purpose flour

3 tablespoons olive oil

3 medium yellow onions, finely chopped

1 pound baby carrots

½ pound celery, thinly sliced

1½ pounds red boiling potatoes, cut into quarters

½ cup cold water

2 tablespoons cornstarch

1 bunch fresh parsley, finely chopped

Salt and freshly ground pepper, to taste

THE DAY BEFORE SERVING, MARINATE THE MEAT: Stir together 3 cups of the broth, the wine, tomatoes, and cloves in a large nonmetal baking dish. Add the beef and turn to coat thoroughly with the marinade. Cover tightly and refrigerate overnight, turning the beef several times and re-covering.

The next day, remove the roast from the marinade. Reserve the marinade, but discard the cloves. Pat the beef dry using paper towels. Place the beef on a sheet of waxed paper on a work surface and sprinkle evenly all over with the salt and pepper. Then turn the beef in the flour until evenly coated, shaking off excess flour.

Preheat the oven to 350F (175C). Place a large (8- to 10-quart) cast-iron Dutch oven over medium-high heat and heat the oil for 1 minute. Add the beef and cook, turning often so it is browned evenly all over.

Pour in the reserved marinade. Add the onions, carrots, celery, and potatoes. The liquid in the Dutch oven should just cover the beef and vegetables to prevent them from cooking dry. (If necessary, add more beef broth to just cover the contents.)

Bring to a simmer, cover tightly, and bake in the lower third of the oven for 2½ hours, checking the pan juices every 30 minutes, adding more beef broth if necessary.

Uncover, and cook 1 to 1½ hours more, or until the beef is fork-tender, basting frequently.

Transfer the beef to a warm deep serving platter, and using a slotted spoon, arrange the vegetables around the beef. Cover and keep warm.

Meanwhile, prepare the sauce: Place the Dutch oven with the liquid over medium-high heat. In a small bowl, whisk together the cold water and cornstarch until the cornstarch has dissolved and the mixture is smooth and well blended. Stir cornstarch mixture and parsley into liquid in the Dutch oven.

Bring to a boil, stirring constantly. Reduce the heat to low, and cook, stirring constantly, until the mixture is glossy and thickened, 2 minutes more.

Taste for seasoning, adding more salt and pepper if necessary. Slice the beef against the grain into thin slices and serve the vegetables and sauce alongside.

NEW MEXICAN POSOLE

POSOLE IS A STEWLIKE SOUP that originated in Jalisco, in the middle of Mexico's Pacific Coast region. It is traditionally served at Christmastime. My time-trimmed version of posole uses canned white hominy, to avoid having to soak the dried to reconstitute it (which adds hours to the recipe preparation). Hominy, a gift to the European settlers from the Native Americans, has a delicious limed-corn taste and slightly chewy texture. Widely available in supermarkets in the South and Southwest, hominy may be more difficult to locate in other regions. You should be able to find canned hominy in Mexican markets. Before I moved to Atlanta from New York City, I used to travel here with an empty suitcase to fill with regional ingredients—among them cans of hominy.

POSOLE

4 tablespoons olive oil

1⅓ pounds lean boneless pork, trimmed and cut into 1-inch cubes

1 pound lean boneless beef chuck, trimmed and cut into 1-inch cubes

2 medium white onions, coarsely chopped

1 quart beef stock or canned beef broth

4 cloves garlic, crushed through a garlic press

3 tablespoons chili powder, or to taste

1 tablespoon dried oregano

3 teaspoons ground cumin

2 teaspoons garlic salt

3 (16-ounce) cans white hominy, drained

Salt and freshly ground pepper, to taste

TOPPINGS

½ cup minced fresh cilantro, to serve

½ cup sliced radishes, to serve

½ cup thinly sliced scallions, to serve

1½ cups (6 ounces) shredded cheddar cheese, to serve

1 cup chopped tomato, to serve

1 cup finely shredded lettuce, to serve

1 lime, cut into 8 wedges, to serve

Heat 2 tablespoons of the oil in a medium (4- to 6-quart) cast-iron Dutch oven over medium-high heat for 1 minute. Add the pork in batches and sear, turning the cubes often so they brown evenly on all sides, 7 to 9 minutes per batch. Transfer the pork to a medium bowl as it is browned and reserve. Add another 1 tablespoon of the oil and repeat the process with the beef, transferring it to the bowl with the pork.

Add the remaining 1 tablespoon oil and the onions and cook, stirring often, until tender, but not browned, 3 minutes.

Pour in the beef stock (caution: mixture will splatter). Stir in the reserved pork and beef until well blended, and bring to a boil. Boil for 1 minute.

Reduce the heat to medium-low and stir in the garlic, chili powder, oregano, cumin, and garlic salt until combined. Simmer, stirring occasionally, until the beef and pork are tender, but not falling apart, 1 to 1½ hours.

Stir in the hominy and heat until hot. Season to taste with salt and pepper. Transfer to a soup tureen and serve with bowls of the toppings to pass at the table.

ROASTED PORK LOIN
WITH CHERRY PAN GRAVY

I USE A ROUND CAKE rack in my cast-iron skillet for a makeshift rack-and-roasting-pan kit. It is the perfect size for a 2½- to 3-pound pork loin. I started roasting pork loin this way years ago in my first Lilliputian apartment, when all I could fit in my kitchen was a skillet and wire cake rack! You can find dried tart red cherries in supermarkets; or order them online from American Spoon Foods.

PORK

> 1 (2½- to 3-pound) boneless pork loin roast, tied
>
> 1 tablespoon olive oil

GRAVY

> ⅓ cup cherry brandy
>
> 1¼ cups canned chicken broth
>
> 2 teaspoons cornstarch
>
> 1½ cups dried tart red cherries
>
> 2 teaspoons minced fresh thyme
>
> Salt and freshly ground pepper, to taste

TO PREPARE THE PORK: Preheat the oven to 350F (175C). Place an 8- to 9-inch-diameter wire cake rack in a large (12- to 14-inch) cast-iron skillet. Put the pork on the rack and brush all over with the oil.

Roast on the center rack of the oven for 1½ to 2 hours or until an instant-read thermometer inserted in the center reaches 160F (70C). Transfer to a platter, cover with foil, and keep warm while you prepare the pan gravy.

TO PREPARE THE GRAVY: Pour off all but 1 tablespoon fat from the skillet, and place the skillet over medium heat. Add the brandy and boil for 30 seconds while scraping up any browned bits stuck to the bottom of the skillet.

Pour the skillet liquid and 1 cup of the chicken broth into a 2- to 3-quart saucepan (not cast iron) and stir until well blended. Set over medium-high heat and bring to a boil. Reduce heat to low and simmer until reduced slightly, 5 minutes.

Meanwhile, in a small cup or bowl, whisk the remaining ¼ cup chicken broth with the cornstarch until well blended. Whisk the cornstarch mixture into the saucepan, bring to a boil, and boil, whisking constantly, until thickened, 1 minute.

Remove the pan from the heat and stir in the cherries and thyme until well blended. Season the sauce with salt and pepper. Serve slices of the pork drizzled with the sauce.

CANADIAN BACON AND PINEAPPLE PIZZA

Makes 1 (12- to 14-inch) pizza; 4 servings

I FIRST SAMPLED A PIZZA like this when I was in Vancouver, during a lunch break before going to the studio for the filming of the cooking show *Cook Off America* of which I was co-host. I remember I was almost late to production that day because I couldn't get enough of this pizza! Weeks later, when I got home, I re-created the concept but added smoked cheese, which makes it all the more marvelous.

DOUGH

1 teaspoon honey or sugar

⅔ cup warm water (110 to 115F; 40 to 45C)

1 (¼-ounce) package active dry yeast

2¼ cups all-purpose flour

½ teaspoon salt

1 tablespoon olive oil, to grease

Cornmeal, to dust

TOPPING

1½ cups homemade or store-bought Alfredo sauce, such as the Contadina brand

12 ounces thinly sliced Canadian bacon, fried until dappled golden brown and cut into bite-sized strips

1½ cups bite-sized fresh pineapple chunks or drained canned pineapple chunks

8 ounces smoked mozzarella cheese or smoked gouda cheese, shredded

TO MAKE THE DOUGH: In a large bowl, dissolve the honey in the water. Sprinkle the yeast over the water and let stand until foamy, about 5 minutes. Using a wooden spoon, stir in 2 cups of the flour and the salt, and stir mixture until it forms a soft dough.

Lightly dust a work surface with the remaining ¼ cup flour. Knead the dough for about 5 minutes until smooth and elastic, incorporating only as much of the flour as necessary to prevent dough from sticking, about 5 minutes. Shape into a ball.

Grease a large, deep bowl with the oil and add the dough. Turn the dough to coat it with the oil. Cover the dough with a kitchen towel and let rise in a warm place until doubled in bulk, about 1 hour. Punch dough down once.

Preheat the oven to 400F (205C). Sprinkle the cornmeal on a greased 14-inch cast-iron pizza pan or a very large (16- to 18-inch) cast-iron skillet.

Roll out the dough on a lightly floured work surface into a 12- to 14-inch round and fit into the pan. Spread the dough evenly with the Alfredo sauce. Sprinkle with the Canadian bacon, followed by the pineapple. Scatter the cheese evenly over all.

Bake the pizza in the lower third of an electric oven or on the floor of a gas oven for 10 to 15 minutes or until crust is golden. Serve at once.

PORK CHOPS WITH HOMEMADE PLUM CHUTNEY

TO ME, PORK AND PLUMS are a marriage made in heaven, and this duo of flavors inspired this dish. The plums provide the foundation for the spiced, slightly tart, glistening, deep-purple chutney—the perfect contrast to the rich pork.

FRESH PLUM CHUTNEY

- 3 tablespoons black currant preserves
- 2 tablespoons cassis vinegar or apple cider vinegar
- 2 tablespoons balsamic vinegar
- 3 tablespoons Dijon mustard
- 1 teaspoon ground cinnamon
- ½ teaspoon ground cloves
- 1½ teaspoons curry powder
- 1 tablespoon sugar
- 1 teaspoon salt
- ½ teaspoon freshly ground pepper
- 2 pounds purple plums, pitted and thinly sliced (7 cups)
- 1 medium red onion, finely chopped

PORK

- 2 tablespoons olive oil, plus more if needed
- 4 (about ¾-inch-thick) pork loin chops (2¼ pounds total)

Preheat the oven to 350F (175C).

TO MAKE THE CHUTNEY: Stir together all the chutney ingredients except the plums and red onion in a medium-sized glass or stainless steel bowl until combined. Then stir in the plums and red onion and reserve until ready to use.

TO PREPARE THE PORK: Heat the oil in a medium (10- to 12-inch) cast-iron skillet over medium-high heat for 2 minutes. Add the pork chops (do not crowd the skillet or overlap the pork pieces) and cook until golden brown, 4 minutes on each side, adding more oil as needed.

Arrange the pork chops in a baking dish (not cast iron) large enough to accommodate them in a single layer, spooning the chutney around and on top.

Bake, uncovered, for 35 to 40 minutes or until the pork is fork-tender and no more pink remains. Serve.

LENTIL PREACHING SOUP

Makes 6 to 8 servings

IN MY RESEARCH OF REGIONAL American cuisine, I have read that lentil soup was served between the Pennsylvania Dutch people's two Sabbath services, hence the name of this basic but wholesome recipe. I've replaced celery and carrots with mushrooms to augment the meaty flavor of the lentils and added celery salt. If you cook the soup with a leftover, meaty ham bone from the butcher or supermarket, even better. A wedge of semi-soft cheese and crusty, whole-wheat bread are the consummate accompaniment.

1 tablespoon olive oil

2 medium yellow onions, finely chopped

4 cloves garlic, crushed through a garlic press

14 ounces white button mushrooms, stemmed and thinly sliced

8 cups chicken stock or canned chicken broth

1 pound dried lentils, picked over and rinsed

14 ounces smoked ham, finely diced (about 4 cups total)

1 tablespoon fresh thyme leaves or 2 teaspoons dried thyme

1½ teaspoons celery salt

1 bay leaf

Salt and freshly ground pepper, to taste

⅓ cup minced fresh parsley

Heat the oil in a medium (4- to 6-quart) cast-iron Dutch oven over medium heat for 2 minutes. Add the onions, garlic, and mushrooms and sauté until the mushrooms just begin to wilt, 8 minutes.

Stir in the chicken stock, lentils, ham, thyme, celery salt, and bay leaf and bring to a boil. Reduce the heat to low and simmer, stirring often, until the lentils are very tender, 1 hour.

Remove and discard the bay leaf. Season the soup with salt and pepper to taste. Stir in the parsley until well blended and serve.

PASTA WITH ROSEMARY-LAMB RAGÙ

Makes 4 servings

THE SLOW SIMMERING MAKES THIS skillet dish easy to make. Simply pour some red wine, pair it with bread, and the meal is complete.

3 tablespoons olive oil

1 medium white onion, finely chopped

3 cloves garlic, crushed through a garlic press

1 pound ground lamb

½ cup dry red wine

1 (28-ounce) can diced tomatoes

1 teaspoon dried rosemary

Salt and freshly ground pepper, to taste

1 pound dry fettuccine pasta

Freshly grated Romano cheese, to serve

Place a large (12- to 14-inch) cast-iron skillet over medium-high heat and heat the oil for 1 minute. Add the onion and garlic and cook, stirring often, until the onion is soft but not browned, 3 to 4 minutes.

Stir in the lamb, breaking up the meat with a wooden spoon. Cook, stirring frequently, just until there is no trace of pink, 5 to 7 minutes.

Stir in the wine and tomatoes. Rub the rosemary between your fingers (to release its aroma) and stir into the skillet.

Reduce the heat to low and simmer, stirring occasionally, until the sauce has thickened, barely any liquid remains, and the flavors are well blended, 30 to 45 minutes. Season with salt and pepper.

Meanwhile, 15 minutes before the sauce is finished: Pour 3 quarts of water into a 6- to 8-quart pot and bring the water to a boil over high heat. Stir in the pasta and return to the boil. Boil, stirring occasionally, until al dente (slightly firm to the bite), 7 to 9 minutes.

Drain the pasta well and divide the pasta among 4 heated plates. Spoon a portion of the sauce over each serving, and serve at once. Pass freshly grated Romano cheese separately.

LAMB CHOPS CROWNED WITH MINT-ARUGULA PESTO

Makes 4 servings (2 chops each)

LEAVE THE STEMS ON THE arugula for this engaging pesto, because much of argula's peppery flavor is concentrated in the stems. However, do remove the stems from the fresh mint sprigs, so it is naturally sweeter and has no astringent bite from the stems.

MINT-ARUGULA PESTO

4 ounces arugula (stems and leaves)

1 cup fresh mint leaves, without stems

1 cup freshly grated Parmesan cheese

5 tablespoons olive oil

2 tablespoons dry white wine

3 cloves garlic, crushed through a garlic press

1 teaspoon salt

½ teaspoon freshly ground pepper

LAMB

2 tablespoons olive oil

8 rib lamb chops (1⅓ to 1½ pounds total)

TO MAKE THE PESTO: Combine all of the pesto ingredients in the bowl of a food processor fitted with the metal blade. Process until the mixture is finely chopped and forms a well-blended paste, about 2 minutes, scraping down the sides of the bowl with a rubber spatula as necessary.

TO COOK THE LAMB: Preheat the oven to 350F (175C). Heat the oil in a large (12- to 14-inch) skillet over medium-high heat for 2 minutes. Add the lamb chops (do not crowd the skillet or let them overlap) and cook until golden brown, 4 minutes on each side.

Transfer the skillet to the oven and bake chops for 5 to 7 minutes for medium-rare (depending on thickness), being careful not to overcook.

Spread the center of each chop with some of the pesto and serve at once. Pass around the rest of the pesto.

CHICKEN AND TURKEY

BEST-EVER BONELESS FRIED CHICKEN WITH BOURBON GRAVY

Makes 4 servings

I KNOW TRADITIONAL FRIED CHICKEN is made with the bones in, but I am smitten with fried chicken (who isn't!) and tired of bones blocking my way to the succulent meat. No bones about it—this is the best I've ever had, and I'm very proud of it. Rather than a white gravy, which is often the gravy of choice, I created a Bourbon Gravy that will make you want to lick the plate. (I have when no one is looking. It is so good I'd probably lick the plate even when someone is looking!) Though there are many passionate disagreements about the best way to fry chicken, generally most Southerners agree that fried chicken *must* be cooked in cast iron. There is even cast-iron cookware manufactured solely for this purpose—a true testament to Americans' adoration of this dish.

CHICKEN

1½ cups all-purpose flour

1½ teaspoons paprika

1½ teaspoons salt

2 teaspoons freshly ground pepper

4 skinless, boneless chicken breast halves (1½ to 1¾ pounds total)

1 cup buttermilk

3 to 5 cups corn oil, to fry

BOURBON GRAVY

1 cup canned chicken broth

3 chicken bouillon cubes dissolved in 1 cup boiling water

¼ cup bourbon

Salt and freshly ground pepper, to taste

TO COOK THE CHICKEN: In a large doubled brown paper bag, combine the flour, paprika, salt, and pepper. Fold over the top of the bag several times to seal tightly and shake until well blended. Reserve 2 tablespoons of the flour mixture for the gravy. Add the chicken and shake gently until evenly coated, then gently shake off any excess.

Pour the buttermilk into a large bowl. Dip each chicken breast half briefly in the buttermilk until well coated, gently shaking off any excess. One by one, return each chicken breast half to the flour mixture and gently shake again until evenly coated.

Place the chicken breast halves on top of another large, flattened brown paper bag and let stand for 10 minutes.

Preheat the oven to 200F (95C). Place a deep, large (12- to 14-inch) cast-iron skillet over medium-high heat, pour enough oil to come halfway up the sides of the skillet, and heat the oil until it tests 350F (175C) on a deep-fry thermometer.

Add the chicken breast halves, cover with a lid, and fry for 4 minutes. Remove the lid and reduce the heat to medium-low and turn the chicken over. Fry, uncovered, until crisp and golden brown and the juices run clear when the chicken is pierced with a fork in the thickest part, 8 to 10 minutes.

Transfer the chicken to a paper towel-lined pan to drain. Remove and discard the paper towels and transfer the pan to the oven to keep the chicken warm until ready to serve.

MEANWHILE, TO PREPARE THE GRAVY: Pour off all the oil from the skillet except 2 tablespoons. Place the skillet over medium-low heat. Stir in the 2 tablespoons reserved flour mixture until well blended, and cook, whisking constantly, for 2 minutes.

Whisk in the chicken broth and the dissolved bouillon mixture. Raise the heat to high and bring to a boil, whisking constantly. Whisk in the bourbon. Cook, whisking constantly, until thickened, 2 minutes more. Season with salt and pepper. Serve the chicken at once and pass the gravy on the side.

CHICKEN FRICASSEE WITH ORZO

Makes 4 servings

I'VE UPDATED THE CLASSIC CHICKEN fricassee in a number of ways. Among them is the use of orzo, found in well-stocked supermarkets and Italian grocery shops. Another is a wonderful convenience product available in the supermarket freezer: frozen mixed vegetables. They come in a variety of mixtures and save shopping and prepping time!

4 skinless, boneless chicken breast halves (1½ to 1¾ pounds total)

½ teaspoon salt

¼ teaspoon freshly ground pepper

3 tablespoons unsalted butter

2 (16-ounce) packages frozen mixed vegetable medleys, such as broccoli, cauliflower, and red bell peppers, thawed

3 cloves garlic, crushed through a garlic press

1 cup canned chicken broth

½ cup dry white vermouth or dry white wine

½ cup heavy cream, at room temperature

1 pound orzo (rice-shaped pasta), cooked according to package directions (6 cups)

Salt and freshly ground pepper, to taste

¼ cup finely chopped fresh parsley

Sprinkle the chicken with the salt and pepper. Melt the butter in a large (12- to 14-inch) cast-iron skillet over medium-high heat. Add the chicken and sauté until golden brown, 3 to 4 minutes on each side (it will be completely cooked later). Transfer the chicken to a plate and reserve.

Place the skillet over medium heat and stir in the mixed vegetables, garlic, broth, and vermouth.

Add the reserved chicken to the skillet and bring to a boil. Cover, reduce heat to low, and simmer for 5 minutes. Flip the chicken over and simmer until the juices run clear when the chicken is pierced with a fork in the thickest part and the vegetables are tender, 10 to 15 minutes.

Remove the chicken from the skillet and keep warm until ready to serve.

Stir the cream into the skillet and raise the heat to medium. Bring to a boil and boil for 3 minutes, stirring. Stir in the cooked orzo and season with salt and pepper.

Using a slotted spoon, divide the orzo-vegetable mixture among the 4 dinner plates, top each with a chicken breast half, sprinkle with the parsley, and serve at once.

Moroccan Spiced-Chicken Couscous

IF YOU DON'T WANT THE slight heat from the amount of cayenne called for, reduce it by half. Moroccan couscous is available at well-stocked supermarkets and health food stores. The roasted red peppers and Greek kalamata olives are available at gourmet stores and most supermarkets.

2 teaspoons garlic powder

1 teaspoon sweet paprika

¾ teaspoon ground cumin

½ teaspoon ground cinnamon

½ teaspoon freshly ground black pepper

¼ teaspoon ground cayenne pepper, or to taste

2 tablespoons olive oil

1 pound chicken breast tenders, thinly sliced crosswise

8 chicken bouillon cubes dissolved in 2¼ cups boiling water

1 (10-ounce) box Moroccan couscous

1 (12-ounce) jar roasted red peppers, drained and cut into thin strips

1 cup pitted Greek kalamata olives, coarsely chopped

⅛ cup fresh lemon juice

Salt and freshly ground black pepper, to taste

Lemon wedges, to serve

Stir together the garlic powder, paprika, cumin, cinnamon, black pepper, cayenne, and oil in a medium bowl until well blended. Stir in the chicken until it's evenly coated with the seasonings.

Transfer the contents of the bowl to a medium (4- to 6-quart) cast-iron Dutch oven and set over medium-high heat. Cook, stirring often, until the chicken is opaque, 5 to 7 minutes.

Add the dissolved chicken bouillon. Bring to a boil, stirring to dissolve all the browned bits on the bottom of the Dutch oven. Stir in the couscous until well distributed and cover with a lid. Remove the Dutch oven from the heat at once, and let stand, covered, for 5 minutes.

Stir in the roasted red peppers, olives, and lemon juice. Season to taste with salt and pepper.

To serve, transfer to a warm serving platter. Fluff lightly with a fork and serve at once. Pass with the lemon wedges to squeeze over the couscous.

THREE-CHEESE CHICKEN CACCIATORE PASTA

Makes 4 servings

CHICKEN CACCIATORE IS DERIVED FROM the Italian *pollo alla cacciatora,* "chicken in the hunter's style," a robust dish of chicken typically cooked with tomatoes, bell peppers, mushrooms, and various aromatics. I have replaced the mushrooms with a trio of cheeses and pasta for an even heartier dish.

1 pound dried farfalle (bow tie pasta)

2 tablespoons olive oil

1 pound skinless, boneless chicken breast halves, cut crosswise into ¼-inch-wide strips

2 medium yellow onions, thinly sliced

2 medium green bell peppers, cut in half lengthwise and thinly sliced

1 (14½-ounce) can stewed tomatoes

2 tablespoons tomato paste

¼ cup red wine vinegar

1 (15-ounce) container ricotta cheese

½ cup freshly grated Asiago or Romano cheese

2 cups (8 ounces) shredded mozzarella cheese

2 large eggs, beaten

1 teaspoon salt

½ teaspoon freshly ground pepper

Bring 3 quarts of water to a boil in a 6- to 8-quart pot over high heat. Stir in the pasta and bring back to the boil. Boil, stirring occasionally, until al dente (slightly firm to the bite), 7 to 9 minutes. Drain the pasta and reserve until ready to use.

Preheat the oven to 350F (175C). Heat the oil in a large (12- to 14-inch) cast-iron skillet over medium-high heat for 1 minute. Add the chicken and cook, stirring occasionally, for 6 minutes or until no longer pink. Remove the chicken and reserve until ready to use.

In the same skillet, cook the onion and bell peppers over medium heat, stirring occasionally, until the onions and peppers are tender, 8 minutes.

Stir in the tomatoes, tomato paste, red wine vinegar, and reserved chicken, and cook, stirring, for 2 minutes.

Remove the skillet from the heat and stir in the reserved pasta until distributed.

Stir together the ricotta cheese, Asiago cheese, mozzarella cheese, eggs, salt, and pepper in a medium bowl until well blended.

Spread the ricotta mixture over the skillet contents in an even layer. Bake for 30 to 35 minutes or until heated through. Serve directly from the skillet.

CHICKEN AND DUMPLINGS

Makes 4 to 6 servings

I FIND THAT MANY PEOPLE don't make honest, old-fashioned chicken and dumplings because they don't own a large enough kettle or sadly, they don't take the time. So here is my answer to this quandary—start out with boneless, skinless chicken breasts rather than a whole chicken. But to put more flavor back into it, use homemade chicken stock, preferably double-strength. Though it is assumed in this cookbook that you will always use a homemade chicken, beef, or vegetable stock over a canned broth or bouillon cubes (neither tend to be as full-flavored as a homemade stock), it is vital to use homemade in this recipe.

DUMPLINGS

3 cups plain soft-wheat flour, such as White Lily or Martha White (see page 170)

½ teaspoon baking soda

½ teaspoon salt

6 tablespoons lard or substitute solid vegetable shortening, chilled

¼ cup homemade chicken stock from your favorite recipe

⅔ cup buttermilk

SOUP

2½ quarts homemade chicken stock from your favorite recipe

10 strips bacon, stacked and cut crosswise into ¼-inch-wide strips

3 bay leaves

1 tablespoon fresh thyme leaves

2½ teaspoons minced fresh sage

¼ teaspoon ground cloves

½ teaspoon salt

½ teaspoon freshly ground black pepper

1 medium white onion, finely chopped

4 carrots, thinly sliced

5 ribs celery, thinly sliced

2 pounds skinless, boneless chicken breast halves

½ cup coarsely chopped fresh parsley

Salt and freshly ground pepper, to taste

To make the dumplings: Combine the flour, baking soda, and salt in a large bowl. Using a fork, stir until well blended. Using a pastry blender or a fork, cut the lard into the flour mixture until it resembles coarse cornmeal. Stir in the chicken stock and buttermilk until well blended and a stiff dough forms. On a lightly floured work surface, knead the dough gently 10 to 12 times. Pat the dough into a flat disk, wrap tightly in plastic wrap, and refrigerate for at least 1 hour, preferably overnight.

To prepare the soup: In a medium (4- to 6-quart) cast-iron Dutch oven over medium-high heat, stir together the chicken stock, bacon, bay leaves, thyme, sage, cloves, salt, and pepper until well blended. Stir in the onion, carrots, and celery.

Bring to a boil. Reduce the heat to medium-low and simmer, stirring occasionally, for 30 minutes.

Add the chicken. Simmer, stirring occasionally, until the chicken is no longer pink in the center, 10 to 15 minutes.

Using a slotted spoon, transfer the cooked chicken to a plate. When cool enough to handle, shred into bite-sized pieces and reserve until ready to use. Remove and discard the bay leaves and raise the heat to medium.

Meanwhile, on a lightly floured work surface, roll out the chilled dough to about ⅛-inch thickness. Sprinkle the dough with more flour if it begins to stick. Cut the dough into 1-inch-wide strips by cutting straight down—do not slide the blade toward you. Cut the strips crosswise to form 1-inch-wide squares.

Drop the dumplings, one at a time, into the simmering soup. As you drop the dumplings into the soup, do not stir. Using a slotted spoon, gently press the dumplings down to submerge them into the liquid.

When all the dumplings are in the soup, simmer until the dumplings are tender but with a slight bite, 10 to 12 minutes. Gently stir in the reserved shredded chicken and the parsley. Season with salt and pepper and serve.

CAROLINA CHICKEN WITH BENNE SEEDS

Makes 4 servings

IT IS THOUGHT THAT AFRICANS aboard slave ships brought sesame seeds to this country for good luck. Sesame seeds, which are grown in the South Carolina Lowcountry, are referred to as "benne seeds." Though this dish has no other kinship to South Carolina beyond this legend, I wanted to create a dish that uses an often overlooked ingredient for entrées—sesame seeds—as a "breading" ingredient for poultry. I suggest serving this simple, invitingly nutty dish with steamed broccoli, perhaps drizzled with a smidgen of melted butter spiked with fresh lemon juice.

4 skinless, boneless chicken breast halves (1½ to 1¾ pounds total)
½ cup buttermilk
¾ cup (3 ounces) sesame seeds
¾ cup unseasoned dry bread crumbs
2 teaspoons dried thyme
1 teaspoon salt
½ teaspoon freshly ground pepper
½ stick (4 tablespoons) unsalted butter, melted
Salt and freshly ground pepper, to taste

Place the chicken in a glass or stainless steel bowl and add the buttermilk. Cover and marinate in the refrigerator at least 30 minutes or up to 2 hours, turning occasionally.

Preheat the oven to 350F (175C). Meanwhile, add the sesame seeds to a medium (10- to 12-inch) cast-iron skillet and set over medium heat. Dry-toast the sesame seeds, tossing, until golden brown, 8 to 12 minutes. Immediately transfer them to a medium bowl.

Stir the bread crumbs, thyme, salt, and pepper into the sesame seeds until well blended.

Lift the chicken breast halves from the marinade, one at a time, and roll in the sesame seed mixture, coating each piece evenly, and arranging in the skillet.

Bake for 25 minutes. Baste with the melted butter and bake for 10 to 15 minutes more or until the juices run clear when the chicken is pierced with a fork in its thickest part. Season with salt and pepper and serve at once.

GREEK-STYLE BAKED CHICKEN WITH FETA AND ARTICHOKES

Makes 4 servings

THIS ENTRÉE I CREATED, REFLECTS a Greek influence in its use of seasonings common to Greece, and is another example of the remarkable versatility of cast iron, as the skillet used can go from cooktop to oven (or vice versa).

3 medium tomatoes, coarsely chopped

2 tablespoons tomato paste

¼ cup dry white wine

2 (12-ounce) jars marinated artichoke hearts, drained and cut into quarters

1½ teaspoons dried oregano

1 teaspoon dried mint

1 teaspoon dried dill weed

½ teaspoon salt

¼ teaspoon freshly ground pepper

2 tablespoons olive oil

4 skinless, boneless, chicken breast halves (1½ to 1¾ pounds total)

4 ounces feta cheese, crumbled

Preheat the oven to 350F (175C). Combine the tomatoes, tomato paste, wine, artichoke hearts, oregano, mint, dill weed, salt, and pepper in a medium glass or stainless-steel bowl and reserve until ready to use.

Place a large (12- to 14-inch) cast-iron skillet over medium heat and heat the oil for 2 minutes. Add the chicken breasts and cook just until golden brown (they will finish cooking in the oven), 3 to 4 minutes on each side.

Ladle the reserved tomato mixture around the chicken in the skillet and bake for 20 minutes.

Top each chicken piece with the feta cheese and return to the oven for 10 minutes more or until the cheese is softened and the juices run clear when the chicken is pierced with a fork in the thickest part. Serve at once.

CHICKEN WITH ARGENTINE CHIMICHURRI

TO SAVE TIME, PURCHASE A bag of pre-shredded coleslaw mixture typically available in the produce case at the supermarket, preferably a mixture of broccoli, carrots, and red cabbage. Or you can shred the vegetables yourself using a food processor fitted with a shredding disk.

Chimichurri is decidedly my favorite quick, no-cook sauce because it is not only full-flavored, but pretty and very versatile. I promise you this piquant sauce will be the new "pesto" of the gourmet world.

CHIMICHURRI SAUCE

⅓ cup olive oil

¼ cup red wine vinegar

½ cup minced onion

½ cup finely chopped fresh parsley

2 cloves garlic, crushed through a garlic press

2 tablespoons minced fresh oregano

¼ teaspoon ground cayenne pepper

Salt and freshly ground pepper, to taste

CHICKEN

3 tablespoons olive oil

1 (16-ounce) bag mixed shredded vegetables, such as broccoli, carrots, and red cabbage

1 cup canned chicken broth

4 skinless, boneless chicken breast halves (1½ to 1¾ pounds total)

TO MAKE THE SAUCE: In a small bowl combine all the sauce ingredients and stir until well blended. Cover and refrigerate for at least 2 hours, preferably overnight, for the flavors to blend. Bring the sauce to room temperature before serving.

TO PREPARE THE CHICKEN: Heat 1 tablespoon of the oil in a large (12- to 14-inch) cast-iron skillet over medium heat for 2 minutes. Add the vegetables and ½ cup of the broth and cook, tossing, until crisp-tender, 5 to 7 minutes. Transfer to a warmed serving platter and keep warm until ready to serve.

Preheat the oven to 350F (175C). Raise the heat under the skillet to medium-high and heat the remaining 2 tablespoons oil for 2 minutes. Add the chicken and cook until golden brown, 3 to 4 minutes on each side.

Add the remaining ½ cup broth and bake the chicken for 25 to 30 minutes or until the juices run clear when the chicken is pierced with a fork in the thickest part.

Place the chicken in the center of the serving platter and surround with the vegetables. Drizzle some of the sauce over all, passing the rest of the sauce at the table. Serve at once.

Cuban Chicken with Pineapple-Rum Sauce

Makes 4 servings

THE PINEAPPLE CHUNKS ADD THE primary flavor to this dinner dish.

½ cup all-purpose flour

½ teaspoon salt

½ teaspoon freshly ground black pepper

1 (2½- to 3-pound) ready-to-cook broiler-fryer chicken, cut up

3 tablespoons olive oil

1 medium white onion, finely chopped

3 cloves garlic, crushed through a garlic press

1 (28-ounce) canned diced tomatoes

1 cup canned chicken broth

¼ cup dark rum

2 tablespoons fresh lime juice

2 teaspoons minced fresh oregano or 1½ teaspoons dried oregano

⅔ cup raisins

1 teaspoon freshly grated lime zest

1 (20-ounce) can pineapple chunks, drained

Hot cooked rice, to serve

In a large bowl, stir together the flour, salt, and pepper until well blended. Turn the chicken parts in the mixture until evenly coated, shaking off any excess.

Place a medium (4- to 6-quart) cast-iron Dutch oven over medium-high heat and heat the oil for 1 minute. Brown the chicken in batches, starting with skin side down, turning often until brown on all sides, 7 to 9 minutes per batch. Transfer the browned chicken to a medium bowl and reserve.

Add the onion, garlic, tomatoes, chicken broth, rum, lime juice, and oregano to the skillet and bring to a boil.

Add the reserved chicken, skin side down, so that the chicken is completely immersed in the cooking liquid. Reduce the heat to medium-low, cover, and simmer for 30 minutes.

Turn the chicken over and stir in the raisins and lime zest. Cover and cook for 10 minutes more.

Stir in the pineapple (make sure the chicken is still completely immersed in the cooking liquid), and cook, uncovered, until the juices run clear when the chicken is pierced with a fork in the thickest part, 10 minutes more.

To serve, remove the chicken with a slotted spoon and place in the center of a warm, heat-proof serving platter, spooning some of the sauce over all. Surround the chicken with hot cooked rice, and pass the remaining sauce separately.

CHICKEN ENCHILADAS

IF TOMATILLOS ARE PLENTIFUL IN your market, you can make your own salsa verde (green salsa), which is typically made of tomatillos, green chiles, and cilantro. Or, you can purchase bottled salsa verde at a supermarket or Mexican market.

E N C H I L A D A S

> 2 tablespoons olive oil
>
> 1 medium white onion, diced
>
> 2 teaspoons minced fresh oregano
>
> Salt and freshly ground pepper, to taste
>
> 6 cups shredded cooked chicken meat (see Cook's Tip below)
>
> 3 tablespoons olive oil, plus more as needed, to fry
>
> 12 (7-inch diameter) flour tortillas
>
> 3 cups (12 ounces) shredded Monterey Jack cheese
>
> 1 (8-ounce) jar salsa verde or 1 cup homemade green salsa
>
> 2 cups heavy cream
>
> 3 large eggs, beaten
>
> Guacamole, sour cream, shredded lettuce, chopped and seeded tomatoes, and chopped and pitted black olives, to serve

Heat the oil in a large (12- to 14-inch) cast-iron skillet over medium-high heat. Add the onion and oregano and season with salt and pepper. Cook, stirring often, until the onion is soft and translucent, 4 minutes.

Remove the skillet from the heat and stir in the shredded cooked chicken until well blended, then transfer the skillet contents to a bowl and reserve until ready to use.

Return the skillet to medium heat and coat the skillet with the 3 tablespoons olive oil. Coating the skillet with more oil as needed, fry the tortillas in batches just until dappled golden brown but still soft and pliable enough to roll, 1 to 2 seconds on each side.

Lay the tortillas on a paper towel-lined work surface to drain. Divide the reserved chicken mixture among the tortillas, placing the chicken mixture on the lower half of each tortilla, spreading it evenly and sprinkling each with about 2 tablespoons of the cheese. Roll up each tortilla into a tube and place, seam side down, in a baking dish large enough to hold the enchiladas in a single layer.

Preheat the oven to 350F (175C). Stir together the salsa, cream, and eggs in a medium bowl until well blended. Pour the cheese mixture over the top of the enchiladas and sprinkle with the remaining cheese.

Bake for 30 to 40 minutes or until heated through and dappled golden brown.

Serve at once with the guacamole, sour cream, lettuce, tomatoes, and olives arranged in colorful rows over the enchiladas.

T I P

> This recipe is a fabulous way to use leftover chicken. Or make the quantity called
> for by cooking 5 to 6 pounds chicken pieces (a combination of breasts, legs, and
> thighs). Remove the skin and bones, and shred the chicken (using 2 forks) to make
> the 6 cups needed for the recipe.

CHICKEN PICCATA WITH WILTED SPINACH

DON'T BE CONCERNED THAT THERE is too much fresh spinach to fit in your skillet, because almost as soon as this garden goodness hits the heat, it wilts, and the shaggy, emerald mass is significantly reduced in size, as if by wizardry.

4 skinless, boneless, chicken breast halves (1½ to 1¾ pounds total)

½ cup all-purpose flour

½ teaspoon salt

¼ teaspoon freshly ground black pepper

½ teaspoon garlic powder

4 tablespoons olive oil

1½ pounds fresh spinach, large stems removed

Salt and freshly ground pepper, to taste

1 stick (½ cup) unsalted butter

Juice of 1 medium lemon

1 tablespoon honey

1 lemon, cut into quarters

On a work surface, place a chicken breast half between 2 sheets of plastic wrap. Using a meat mallet, pound from the center of the chicken toward the outer edge, rotating 180 degrees about every 5 strikes, until the chicken is flattened to an even ½-inch thickness.

Repeat the process with remaining chicken, reusing plastic wrap if not punctured. Peel off the plastic wrap and cut each pounded chicken piece in half lengthwise.

Combine the flour, salt, pepper, and garlic powder in a shallow dish.

Dip each chicken piece into the flour mixture until coated evenly, shaking off any excess, and transfer to a piece of waxed paper.

Heat 3 tablespoons of the oil in a large (12- to 14-inch) cast-iron skillet over medium-high heat for 2 minutes. Add the chicken and cook until browned evenly and juices run clear when pierced with a fork in the thickest part, 3 to 4 minutes on each side.

Transfer the chicken to a serving platter and keep warm until ready to serve.

Place the skillet with its juices over medium-high heat. Add the remaining 1 tablespoon oil and heat for 1 minute. Add the spinach, season with salt and pepper, and cook, stirring, just until wilted, 1 minute. Transfer to the serving platter and arrange spinach beneath and around the chicken; keep warm.

Working quickly, place the skillet over low heat. Melt the butter and stir in the lemon juice and honey. Drizzle over the chicken and season with salt and pepper. Serve at once with the lemon quarters to squeeze over the chicken.

LIME-TEQUILA GRILL-PAN CHICKEN

Makes 4 servings

FOODIES ACROSS THE NATION WHO are stuck in tiny apartments with no backyard or outdoor grill love using a cast-iron ridged grill pan because it enables them to achieve the lovely "grill mark" look. Those of us who are blessed with an outdoor grill also love our cast-iron ridged grill pan because we can still grill even when it rains.

If you have a favorite homemade salsa, you can use that in place of the prepared tomato salsa. Though there are some excellent tomato salsas on the market nowadays, I have used a range of different salsas with this dish from black bean to pineapple and mango, all with great results.

4 skinless, boneless chicken breast halves (1½ to 1¾ pounds total)
¼ cup plus 1 tablespoon olive oil
¼ cup fresh lime juice
¼ cup tequila
3 tablespoons honey
⅓ cup store-bought chunky-style tomato salsa, to serve
⅛ cup minced fresh cilantro, to serve

Place the chicken pieces on a piece of waxed paper. Using the 1 tablespoon oil, coat the chicken evenly on both sides and reserve at room temperature until ready to use or up to 30 minutes.

In a medium glass or stainless steel bowl, whisk together the ¼ cup oil, lime juice, tequila, and honey; set aside.

Place a 10- to 12-inch-square cast-iron ridged grill pan over medium-high heat and heat for about 2 minutes, or until a drop of water dances on its surface.

Cook the chicken until striped grill marks form on the bottom, 5 to 6 minutes. Flip the chicken over and cook until the juices run clear when the chicken is pierced with a fork in the thickest part, 5 to 6 minutes more.

Immediately pour the tequila mixture (caution: it will splatter) over the chicken and cook 1 minute to allow the alcohol in the tequila to burn off (otherwise it can lend a bitter flavor). Serve the chicken at once, drizzled with the pan juices and topped with the salsa and the cilantro.

Shaker-Style Chicken in Cider and Cream

THE SHAKERS ARE KNOWN FOR their resourcefulness and their ability to make an exquisite thing of beauty with very little. This is certainly seen in their handicrafts, and I have learned it is often replicated in their cuisine. A few simple American-born ingredients, when precisely combined, create something surprising in its complexity and altogether different in the end. In this recipe, the chicken is cloaked in a light cream sauce that has a tang of apple and a very slight bite of the apple vinegar—almost a sweet-sour effect, not startling to the tongue, just wonderfully provocative.

½ stick (¼ cup) unsalted butter

4 skinless, boneless chicken breast halves (1½ to 1¾ pounds total)

⅔ cup apple cider or apple juice

⅓ cup apple cider vinegar

1 cup heavy cream, at room temperature

Salt and freshly ground pepper, to taste

¼ cup minced fresh parsley

Granny Smith apple, unpeeled, thinly sliced, to garnish

Preheat the oven to 350F (175C). In a large (12- to 14-inch) cast-iron skillet over medium-high heat, melt the butter. Add the chicken and sauté until golden brown, 5 to 7 minutes on each side.

Transfer the skillet to the oven and bake, covered, for 20 to 30 minutes, or until the juices run clear when the chicken is pierced with a fork in the thickest part.

Meanwhile, place a 3- to 4-quart saucepan (not cast iron) over medium-high heat. Add the cider and vinegar and boil until reduced by about one-fourth, 3 to 5 minutes.

Gradually whisk in the cream until well blended. Bring to a boil. Boil, whisking frequently, until thickened, 4 minutes. Season with salt and pepper.

Divide the chicken among the dinner plates, ladle with the sauce, and sprinkle evenly with the parsley. Garnish each plate with a fan of apple slices, and serve at once.

COUNTRY CAPTAIN

Makes 4 servings

THE CAMPS ARE DIVIDED AS to the roots of this mouthwatering recipe. Some culinary historians believe that the dish got its name from a British army officer who brought the recipe back from his station in India. Others contend that the dish originated in Savannah, Georgia, a major shipping port for the spice trade. After delving in to the matter, all I can add is that once I tasted Country Captain during a stay in Savannah, I have never forgotten it. Now you, too, can partake.

1 (2.5-ounce) bag sliced almonds (½ cup total), to serve

3 tablespoons olive oil

4 skinless, boneless chicken breast halves (1½ to 1¾ pounds total)

2 medium yellow onions, thinly sliced

2 green bell peppers, cut lengthwise then thinly sliced

2 cloves garlic, crushed through a garlic press

3 ribs celery, thinly sliced

1 tablespoon curry powder, or to taste

½ teaspoon dried thyme

2 (14½-ounce) cans stewed tomatoes

Salt and freshly ground pepper, to taste

Hot cooked rice, to serve

½ cup dried zante currants (available at supermarkets or health food stores), to serve

Mango chutney, to serve

Add the almonds to a medium (4- to 6-quart) cast-iron Dutch oven and place over medium heat. Dry-toast the almonds, tossing, until golden brown, 5 to 7 minutes. Transfer to a bowl and reserve until ready to use.

Return the Dutch oven to medium heat and heat the oil for 2 minutes. Add the chicken and sauté until golden brown, 6 to 8 minutes on each side. Transfer the chicken to a plate and set aside.

Place the Dutch oven over medium-low heat and add the onions, bell peppers, garlic, and celery and cook, stirring often, until soft, about 5 minutes.

Reduce the heat to low and stir in the curry powder, thyme, and tomatoes. Return the chicken to the Dutch oven and immerse in the sauce so it is completely covered. Cover and simmer for 15 minutes. Turn the chicken over; cover and cook until the chicken is tender and no more pink remains, 15 minutes. Season with salt and pepper.

To serve, spoon the hot cooked rice onto a serving platter, top with the chicken, and then top with the sauce. Sprinkle with the reserved toasted almonds, then the currants, and serve with the mango chutney.

T I P

When using dried herbs, make sure to rub the leaves between your fingers while adding them to the dish to release their full flavor.

BAKED TURKEY RIGATONI WITH MARJORAM AND RICOTTA

Makes 4 to 6 servings

RIGATONI IS A FAIRLY SHORT, grooved, tubular pasta that is a perfect choice to trap the surprisingly delicately flavored, enticing marjoram-scented turkey mixture of this dish—which is even better the next day.

Pancetta is an Italian bacon that is cured with salt and spices but not smoked. It comes in a sausagelike roll and must be well-sliced and/or chopped and cooked. It is available in well-stocked supermarkets.

1½ teaspoons salt

1 pound dry rigatoni

¼ pound pancetta, thinly sliced and coarsely chopped

2 medium yellow onions, finely chopped

1⅓ pounds ground turkey

½ cup dry white wine

1 (28-ounce can) diced tomatoes

2 teaspoons minced fresh marjoram or 2 teaspoons dried marjoram

¼ teaspoon freshly ground pepper

1 (32-ounce) container ricotta cheese

1 cup freshly grated Parmesan or Romano cheese

Bring 3 quarts of water and 1 teaspoon of the salt to a boil in a 6- to 8-quart pot over high heat. Add the pasta to the pot and stir the pasta at once. Boil, stirring occasionally, until al dente (slightly firm to the bite), 7 to 9 minutes. Drain in a colander and reserve until ready to use.

Meanwhile, in a large (12- to 14-inch) cast-iron skillet over medium heat, cook the pancetta until it is slightly crisp, about 2 minutes. Stir in the onions and the turkey, breaking up the turkey with a wooden spoon. Cook, stirring often, just until the turkey has no trace of pink, 5 to 7 minutes.

Stir in the wine and tomatoes. Rub the marjoram between your fingers (to release its aroma) and stir into the skillet along with the ½ teaspoon salt and pepper until well blended. Cook, stirring occasionally, about 3 minutes.

Preheat the oven to 350F (175C). Stir together the ricotta and Parmesan cheese in a medium bowl.

Ladle half of the turkey mixture evenly over the bottom of a 13 × 9-inch baking dish. Spoon half of the rigatoni over the turkey mixture. Using the back of a wooden spoon, press down gently to flatten. Dot evenly with half of the ricotta mixture. Spread with the remaining turkey mixture, followed by the remaining rigatoni and the ricotta mixture.

Bake for 30 to 40 minutes to heat through and allow the flavors to blend. Let stand for 10 minutes before serving. Serve hot directly from the baking dish.

ROAST TURKEY BREAST WITH QUINCE GLAZE

Makes 6 servings

QUINCE TASTES LIKE A CROSS between a tart apple and a pear and is a good match to full-flavored roasted turkey.

6¾-pound turkey breast (with ribs, portions of wing meat, and skin and back attached)

½ stick (¼ cup) unsalted butter, melted

⅓ cup quince preserves, such as Hero brand (available from gourmet stores)

Preheat the oven to 350F (175C). Place the turkey breast, meat side up, in a medium (4- to 6-quart) cast-iron Dutch oven.

Roast for 1½ to 2½ hours (15 to 20 minutes per pound). During the last 10 minutes of cooking time, baste with the melted butter. The breast is done when an instant-read thermometer inserted in the thickest part reads 160F (70C).

Transfer the turkey breast from the Dutch oven to a serving platter. Brush the surface of the turkey with the quince preserves until evenly coated. (The heat of the turkey will melt the preserves to form a glaze.)

Let stand for 15 minutes before serving for easier carving. Serve warm.

MONTE CRISTO SANDWICHES

A KNIFE-AND-FORK SANDWICH, this American classic, dipped in a French toast–like batter and grilled until the exterior is golden and crisp, sings when cooked on cast iron. But that's true for any grilled sandwiches! Though this is completely my newfangled idea, you *must* try this with maple syrup. It is delicious with honey, too, and makes for a perfect brunch dish.

8 slices white sandwich bread

2 teaspoons Dijon mustard

8 ounces roasted turkey, thinly sliced

8 ounces smoked ham, thinly sliced

8 ounces Swiss cheese, thinly sliced

4 large eggs

½ cup milk

¼ teaspoon salt

½ stick (4 tablespoons) unsalted butter

Maple syrup, to serve

For each sandwich, lay the bread slices out on a work surface; spread 4 of the slices with ½ teaspoon of mustard each. Top the 4 mustard-coated slices with ¼ of each of the turkey, ham, and cheese, then cover with the second bread slice, pressing down gently to close.

Whisk together the eggs, milk, and salt in a medium bowl until well blended.

Melt the butter in a large (12- to 14-inch) cast-iron skillet over medium heat.

Dip each sandwich in the batter, turning it briefly to allow the batter to be absorbed. Cook the sandwiches until golden brown, crispy on the outside, and the cheese has melted, 2 to 4 minutes on each side. Cut each sandwich in half on the diagonal to form 2 triangular pieces and serve at once drizzled with maple syrup.

FISH, SHELLFISH, AND CHEESE

PAN-FRIED CATFISH

LEMON SOLE WITH A POTATO CRUST

GINGER-CRUSTED TUNA NIÇOISE

SALMON CAKES WITH GARLIC TARTAR SAUCE ON WATERCRESS

SMOKED SALMON AND SCALLION-CREAM CHEESE QUESADILLAS

PASTA WITH CAULIFLOWER SAUCE

CHINESE-AMERICAN SHRIMP CHOW MEIN

OKONOMIYAKI

SHRIMP GUMBO WITH FILÉ

THAI-STYLE "PAELLA"

PASTA CAPONATA

LINGUINE WITH WHITE CLAM SAUCE

SEARED SEA SCALLOP, SPINACH, AND STRAWBERRY SALAD
WITH AMBROSIAL VINAIGRETTE

LEMONGRASS-SCENTED SHRIMP WITH JASMINE RICE

PASTA PUTTANESCA

SPAGHETTI PIE WITH PESTO AND VEGETABLE MEDLEY

ITALIAN PASTA É FAGIOLI

BROCCOLI RABE WITH ORECCHIETTE, GARLIC, AND CRUSHED RED PEPPER

PAN-FRIED CATFISH

Makes 4 servings

IN SOUTHERN FOOD LEXICON, CATFISH is nearly always fried, and you certainly need a trusty, seasoned, good ole cast-iron skillet to fry it. Old Bay Seasoning is available in supermarkets; alternatively I have given you a recipe for a homemade "copy-cat" of this well-known seasoning blend.

> 4 (5- to 6-ounce) catfish fillets
>
> 1 teaspoon salt
>
> ½ teaspoon freshly ground pepper
>
> 1 cup white cornmeal
>
> 1 tablespoon plus 1 teaspoon Old Bay Seasoning or substitute "copy-cat" Old Bay Seasoning Blend (page 79)
>
> ½ teaspoon celery salt
>
> ¼ teaspoon ground cayenne pepper
>
> 7 to 9 cups vegetable oil, to fry
>
> 1 lemon, cut into 4 wedges
>
> Fresh parsley sprigs, to garnish

Season both sides of the catfish with the salt and pepper. Place the cornmeal, Old Bay Seasoning, celery salt, and cayenne in a large, plastic resealable bag. One at a time, place the fillets in the bag, seal, and shake the bag gently until the fish is thoroughly and evenly coated with cornmeal.

Pour the oil into a medium (4- to 6-quart) cast-iron Dutch oven to a depth of 3 inches and set over medium heat. Heat the oil until it registers 360F (180C) on a deep-fry thermometer.

Fry the fillets in one batch until the catfish is golden brown on both sides and opaque throughout, 3 to 4 minutes on each side. Check often for doneness to prevent overcooking. Drain on paper towels and serve at once with lemon wedges and parsley garnish.

"COPY-CAT" OLD BAY SEASONING BLEND

1 tablespoon ground bay leaves (grind 4 to 5 whole bay leaves—or enough to make
1 tablespoon once ground—in an electric spice grinder until finely ground)

2½ teaspoons celery salt

1½ teaspoons dry mustard

1½ teaspoons black pepper

¾ teaspoon ground nutmeg

½ teaspoon ground cloves

½ teaspoon ground ginger

½ teaspoon paprika

½ teaspoon ground cayenne pepper

¼ teaspoon ground mace

In a small bowl, combine all ingredients, and stir until well blended.

Transfer to a clean, dry, airtight glass container. Store up to 3 months away from heat,
light, or moisture.

LEMON SOLE WITH A POTATO CRUST

POTATO-CRUSTED DISHES ARE VERY POPULAR in restaurants, but the technique can be tricky. I created this rustic version to be enjoyed at home—imagine the flavor of fish and chips. It works well with catfish fillets, as long as the fillets chosen are boneless. I find that for this recipe, using an old-fashioned four-sided box grater with large holes works better for grating the potatoes into shreds than a food processor because the shreds are thinner and lighter when prepped with the grater.

1 cup all-purpose flour

1 teaspoon salt

½ teaspoon freshly ground pepper

1 large egg

½ cup milk

1 pound baking potatoes

4 lemon sole fillets or other firm, white-fleshed fish fillets (½ to ¾ pound total)

½ cup olive oil

¼ cup minced fresh parsley, to garnish

Garlic Tartar Sauce (page 84) or store-bought bottled tartar sauce, to serve

Stir together the flour, salt, and pepper until well blended in a wide bowl.

Using a whisk, beat the egg with the milk in another wide bowl.

Peel the potatoes and grate them on the large holes of a 4-sided box grater into a shallow pan, spreading the grated potatoes out.

Dredge the fillets, one at a time, in the flour mixture until evenly coated all over, shaking off any excess. Dip the fillets, one at a time, in the egg mixture, and then into the grated potatoes, gently but firmly pressing the potatoes onto both sides of the fillets so the potatoes will stick. Transfer the potato-crusted fillets to a piece of waxed paper.

Heat the oil in a large (12- to 14-inch) cast-iron skillet over medium-high heat for 2 minutes. Using a wide, metal spatula, carefully lift the potato covered fillets and place them in the hot oil. Cook the fillets until golden brown and the potatoes are crisp, 4 to 6 minutes on each side. (When the potatoes have formed a golden crust, the fillets will release from the skillet bottom. Use a spatula to help loosen them if necessary.) If the potatoes appear to be cooking too quickly, reduce the heat to medium, so as not to burn the potatoes, and test to make sure the fish is opaque.

Place each fillet on a plate, sprinkle with parsley, spoon the tartar sauce alongside the fillets, and serve at once.

GINGER-CRUSTED TUNA NIÇOISE

Makes 4 servings

I HAVE USED THE BASIS of a traditional niçoise salad (with the exception of anchovies) and added such Asian influences as a ginger crust to the tuna and a mirin dressing to the salad. The green beans, potatoes, and eggs, as well as the tuna, are cooked ahead so they may be served once they reach room temperature. Do warn your guests that the tiny niçoise olives have pits (they are too small to pit) and that it is proper etiquette to discretely remove pits at the table while they enjoy their salad. Because of its make ahead quality and its satisfying makeup, I serve this as a summer supper salad for elegant dinner parties.

DRESSING

¼ cup soy sauce

¼ cup plus 1 tablespoon mirin (Japanese rice wine), available from health food store or Japanese grocery shop

⅛ cup olive oil

TUNA

½ cup unseasoned dry bread crumbs (available at the supermarket)

1 tablespoon cream-style horseradish or prepared horseradish

1 tablespoon Dijon mustard

1 tablespoon mirin

1 tablespoon plus 1 teaspoon freshly grated peeled fresh ginger

¾ teaspoon salt

½ teaspoon freshly ground pepper

1 tablespoon olive oil

2 pounds tuna steaks

SALAD

¾ pound fresh green beans, trimmed, cooked until crisp-tender

1 (4-ounce) head Boston lettuce, cored, leaves separated

1 pint cherry tomatoes

1 pound small boiling potatoes, unpeeled, cooked until tender, and cut into quarters

¾ cup niçoise olives

4 eggs, hard-cooked and cut into quarters

To make the dressing: In a small bowl whisk together the soy sauce, mirin, and oil until well blended and reserve the dressing until ready to use.

To prepare the tuna: Stir together the bread crumbs, horseradish, mustard, mirin, ginger, salt, and pepper in a medium bowl.

Place a large (12- to 14-inch) cast-iron skillet over medium heat. Add the oil and heat for 2 minutes. Arrange the tuna in a single layer; do not crowd the skillet or overlap the tuna steaks. Cook for 5 minutes on the first side.

Reduce the heat to medium-low. Turn the tuna steaks, and using a spatula or the back of a wooden spoon, press the bread crumb mixture in an even layer onto the top of each tuna steak.

Cover with a lid and cook until opaque throughout, 4 to 5 minutes more (do not turn over again).

Using a spatula, transfer to a plate and reserve, allowing to come to room temperature.

To make the salad: In a medium bowl, toss together the green beans with several tablespoons of the reserved dressing. Line 4 large dinner plates with the lettuce leaves.

Decoratively arrange the bean mixture, tomatoes, potatoes, olives, and eggs in individual groups on the lettuce. Slice the tuna into ½-inch-wide strips and arrange on the salads.

Drizzle the remaining reserved dressing over the composed salads (but not on the tuna so as not to disturb its coating) and serve.

SALMON CAKES WITH GARLIC TARTAR SAUCE ON WATERCRESS

Makes 4 servings (4 cakes each)

THIS RECIPE IS CULLED FROM my cookbook *Onions: A Celebration of Onions Through Recipes, Lore, and History.* I had to include it in this tome on cast-iron cookery because these seafood cakes are at their very best when cooked in a cast-iron skillet.

GARLIC TARTAR SAUCE

- ¾ cup mayonnaise
- ¾ cup sour cream
- 3 tablespoons Dijon mustard
- 3 tablespoons sweet pickle relish
- 3 tablespoons capers, finely chopped
- 5 cloves garlic, crushed through a garlic press

SALMON CAKES

- ½ cup minced celery
- ½ cup very thinly sliced scallions, including the greens
- 1 cup dry unseasoned bread crumbs
- 1 tablespoon finely chopped fresh dill
- 2 teaspoons Dijon mustard
- ½ teaspoon salt
- 1 teaspoon freshly ground pepper
- 3 dashes hot pepper sauce
- ⅛ teaspoon ground nutmeg
- 2 large egg whites
- 2 salmon steaks, about 8 ounces each, cooked, cooled, skin and bones discarded, and flaked into medium pieces
- 3 tablespoons vegetable oil, plus more if needed, to fry
- 2 bunches watercress, trimmed, washed well, and dried

TO MAKE THE TARTAR SAUCE: Combine all the sauce ingredients in a medium glass or stainless steel bowl and stir until well blended. Cover and refrigerate until serving. Serve chilled. (This sauce is best made 1 day ahead of serving to allow the flavors to blend.)

To prepare the salmon cakes: Combine the celery, scallions, bread crumbs, dill, mustard, salt, pepper, hot pepper sauce, and nutmeg in a medium bowl until well blended. Stir in the egg whites just until mixture is moistened, then fold in the salmon until well distributed. The mixture should be moist enough to stick together. (If mixture is too moist to work with, refrigerate it for 15 minutes before forming into patties.)

Using your hands, squeeze the mixture into 16 compact, evenly sized balls. Using your palm, flatten each ball into a patty 2 inches in diameter, making the patties as uniform and flat as possible. Do not overwork or the cakes will be dry. (If you aren't cooking the cakes right away, place on a baking sheet, cover loosely with plastic wrap, and refrigerate up to 4 hours.)

Preheat the oven to 200F (95C). Heat 1½ tablespoons of the oil in a large (12- to 14-inch) cast-iron skillet over medium-high heat. Add half of the cakes and fry until browned, 2 to 3 minutes on each side, adding a little more oil if needed, and using a spatula to flatten slightly while cooking.

Drain briefly on paper towels. Transfer the cakes to a baking sheet and hold in the warm oven while cooking the second batch. Heat the remaining oil for 1 minute before adding the second batch and fry as you did the first batch.

Line 4 plates with the watercress. Top with the hot salmon cakes and pass the chilled tartar sauce.

Smoked Salmon and Scallion-Cream Cheese Quesadillas

Makes 4 servings (3 quesadillas each)

I HAVE AN AFFINITY FOR quesadillas and am always experimenting with new ways to prepare them. When I discovered the amazing results when tortillas are fried in a cast-iron skillet or griddle, my repertoire expanded to include this delight of a swift dish. I like to serve these for brunch, holding them in the oven until all the guests are seated and I'm ready to serve them family-style on a large pottery platter or on individual plates. Smoked salmon, cream cheese, and scallions tucked between a warm tortilla is great to quell the pangs of hunger any time of the day because they are as easy to make for one as they are for twenty-one.

> 12 (7-inch-diameter) flour tortillas
>
> 1 (8-ounce) package cream cheese
>
> 4 scallions, very thinly sliced
>
> 8 ounces sliced smoked salmon, cut into ¼-inch-wide strips
>
> 4 tablespoons olive oil, to fry
>
> Tomato salsa, to serve
>
> Guacamole, to serve

Lay the tortillas out on a work surface. Divide and spread the cream cheese among them to cover half of each tortilla completely, leaving a ¼-inch border of uncovered tortilla around the edges.

Divide and sprinkle the scallions and salmon strips evenly over the cheese and fold each tortilla in half, pressing firmly to seal.

Preheat the oven to 200F (95C). Coat a large (12- to 14-inch) cast-iron skillet or griddle with 1 tablespoon of the olive oil. Heat over medium-high heat for 1 minute. Depending on the size of the skillet, add 3 or 4 quesadillas, but do not overlap or crowd the skillet.

Fry until the tortillas are golden brown and crispy, 1 to 3 minutes, using a spatula to gently press each tortilla down. Flip over and fry on the other side until tortillas are golden and crispy, 1 to 3 minutes.

Add another 1 tablespoon of oil and repeat the process until you have used all the tortillas; hold the cooked quesadillas in the warm oven.

To serve, cut each tortilla into 2 wedges and serve at once with a spoonful of tomato salsa and guacamole.

PASTA WITH CAULIFLOWER SAUCE

YEARS AGO A FRIEND MADE this dish, which she had eaten during a visit to Sicily, for me. This is a complexly flavored dish, which I find remarkable given the fact that there are so few ingredients. The combination of flavors, textures, the white of the cauliflower, and the faint seafood flavor from the anchovies makes the resulting taste reminiscent of a white clam sauce.

1 (2½- to 2¾-pound) head cauliflower, cored and separated into florets

1 pound dry conchiglie (shell-shaped pasta)

6 tablespoons extra-virgin olive oil

5 cloves garlic, crushed through a garlic press

5 anchovy fillets, minced

12 ounces provolone cheese, shredded

¼ cup minced fresh parsley

Salt and freshly ground pepper, to taste

⅓ cup capers, drained, to garnish

Bring 3 quarts of water to a boil in a 6- to 8-quart pot over high heat. Add the cauliflower and boil until crisp-tender, 5 to 7 minutes. Drain well in a colander and rinse under cold running water to cool the cauliflower.

Transfer the cauliflower to a cutting board, finely chop, and reserve.

Meanwhile, bring 3 quarts of water to a boil in a 6- to 8-quart pot over high heat. Stir in the pasta and return to the boil. Boil until al dente (slightly firm to the bite), stirring occasionally, 7 to 9 minutes.

Place a large (12- to 14-inch) cast-iron skillet over medium heat and heat 3 tablespoons of the oil for 1 minute. Add the reserved cauliflower and sauté until fork-tender and heated throughout, 4 to 6 minutes.

Add 2 tablespoons more of the oil, the garlic, and the anchovies and sauté for 2 minutes more.

Working quickly, drain the pasta well and transfer to a heated deep serving bowl and toss with the remaining 1 tablespoon oil, the sauce, the provolone, and the parsley until well coated. Season to taste with salt and pepper, sprinkle with the capers, and serve at once.

CHINESE-AMERICAN SHRIMP CHOW MEIN

YOU CAN PURCHASE CHOW MEIN noodles at the supermarket, where you'll find both the thin, crispy variety and also a wider, crispy type. The crunchiness of the noodles against the stir-fry topping is very stimulating to the palate due to the textural contrasts. As you enjoy the dish, you'll find that the noodles soften slightly from the natural juices of the dish. The dried black winter mushrooms called for, are available in Asian markets and health food stores.

1 (1-pound head) bok choy, tough outer leaves removed and discarded

1 tablespoon soy sauce

⅔ cup canned chicken broth

¼ teaspoon salt

¼ teaspoon freshly ground pepper

2 tablespoons cornstarch

3 tablespoons peanut oil

1 medium yellow onion, finely chopped

8 dried black winter mushrooms, soaked in ½ cup warm water for 20 minutes, drained, squeezed gently to remove excess water, and thinly sliced, or 8 ounces white button, mushrooms, stemmed and thinly sliced

4 ounces fresh snow peas, stems and strings removed and cut in half crosswise on the diagonal

1 (8-ounce) can sliced water chestnuts, drained

8 ounces fresh mung bean sprouts

1 pound shelled, cooked shrimp

1 (13-ounce) package chow mein noodles, cooked according to package directions and drained

3 scallions, white and green parts, cut on the diagonal into 1-inch-long pieces, to garnish

Trim off the root end and separate the leaves of the bok choy. Wash thoroughly, drain, and pat dry with paper towels. Cut each bok choy leaf in half lengthwise, then cut each piece crosswise into 1-inch-long pieces and reserve until ready to use.

Combine the soy sauce, chicken broth, salt, pepper, and cornstarch in a small bowl. Stir until the cornstarch is completely dissolved and the mixture is well blended and smooth. Reserve until ready to use.

Add the oil to a cast-iron wok, rotating the wok to coat the sides, and heat over medium-high heat until the oil is rippling, about 1½ minutes.

Add the onion and stir-fry (caution: oil will splatter), tossing quickly until aromatic but not browned, about 30 seconds.

Add the bok choy and mushrooms and stir-fry until the bok choy is crisp tender and the mushrooms are tender, 2 to 3 minutes.

Add the snow peas, water chestnuts, and bean sprouts. Stir-fry, tossing gently, until the snow peas are crisp-tender, about 2 minutes.

Stir the reserved soy sauce mixture to recombine, then gradually stir it into the wok. Cook, stirring constantly, until the sauce thickens and coats the mixture with a glossy coating, about 1 minute. Stir in the shrimp and stir-fry just until the shrimp is heated through, 10 seconds.

Remove the wok from the heat and serve at once over the chow mein noodles. Garnish with the scallions.

Okonomiyaki

NEVER TO BE ONE TO leave well enough alone, I've adapted the ingenious recipe for Okonomiyaki (Japanese pizza) from the chapter by Andi Gladstone in the *Sundays at Moosewood Restaurant* cookbook by the Moosewood Collective. I suggest using a food processor fitted with a shredding disk to shred the cabbage and carrots. Nori is paper-thin sheets of dried seaweed. If you purchase it plain you will need to toast it as described in the method below. Or you can purchase nori pre-toasted; the label will read *yakinori*.

1 (8 × 7-inch) sheet nori (available at Asian markets or health food stores)

¼ cup ketchup

2 tablespoons bottled teriyaki sauce

2 teaspoons mirin (Japanese rice wine) (available at Asian markets or health food stores)

1 cup all-purpose flour

1 cup water

2 large eggs, beaten

¼ teaspoon salt

2 cups shredded green cabbage

½ cup shredded carrot

4 whole scallions, each cut in half lengthwise and then crosswise into 1-inch pieces

4 tablespoons vegetable oil

1 cup thinly sliced cooked crabmeat

Using long-handled tongs to hold it flat and wearing long flameproof oven mitts, carefully with caution, toast each sheet of nori by holding it 5 inches above a low gas flame until the nori stiffens slightly, 10 to 20 seconds on each side (it burns easily). Using your fingers, tear the nori into bite-sized pieces and reserve.

To make the sauce, stir together the ketchup, teriyaki sauce, and mirin in a small bowl until well blended. Reserve until ready to use.

Stir together the flour, water, eggs, and salt until it's the consistency of pancake batter. Stir in the cabbage, carrot, and scallions until well blended.

Preheat the oven to 200F (95C). Heat 1 tablespoon of the vegetable oil in a medium (10- to 12-inch) cast-iron skillet over medium heat for 1 minute.

Spoon one-fourth of the batter onto the hot skillet and spread, making sure the vegetables are evenly distributed. Then sprinkle one-fourth of the crabmeat on top.

Cook over medium heat until lightly browned, 2 minutes. Turn and cook the other side for 2 minutes. Reduce the heat to low and cook, covered, for another 5 minutes, occasionally turning and gently pressing the okonomiyaki with a wooden or metal spatula. Repeat the process with the remaining vegetable oil and batter to make a total of 4 pancakes.

Hold the finished pancakes in the warm oven while making the remaining, or use 2 skillets and make 2 okonomiyaki at a time.

Drizzle 1 tablespoon sauce on each okonomoyaki and top with a sprinkling of the reserved toasted nori. Serve at once.

SHRIMP GUMBO WITH FILÉ

I'VE USED SEVERAL SHORTCUTS TO make this gumbo, among them using mixed vegetable juice and frozen sliced okra and toasting the flour first, rather than cooking a roux (a mixture of flour and fat used as a base to thicken sauces and soups) for a lengthy time to make the fuller-flavored, deep golden brown roux with its nutty flavor, characteristic of Gumbos. When you follow the instructions below for toasting flour, make sure to turn on your exhaust fan.

¼ cup all-purpose flour

6 strips bacon, diced

1 large white onion, finely chopped

3 cloves garlic, crushed through a garlic press

5 ribs celery, finely chopped

3 medium green bell peppers, finely chopped

2 cups canned vegetable broth

1 (10-ounce) package frozen sliced okra, thawed

1 (10-ounce) package frozen corn kernels, thawed

1 tablespoon fresh thyme leaves or 1½ teaspoons dried thyme

⅛ teaspoon ground cayenne pepper

2 pounds medium shrimp, shelled and deveined

1 (14½-ounce) can stewed tomatoes

3 cups canned mixed vegetable juice

¼ cup finely chopped fresh parsley

1½ to 2 teaspoons filé powder (ground dried sassafras leaves), moistened in 2 tablespoons water, available in gourmet shops and many supermarkets

Hot cooked rice, to serve

Hot red pepper sauce, to serve

Add the flour to a small (6- to 8-inch) cast-iron skillet and set over medium heat. Dry-toast, stirring constantly, until the flour is golden brown (the color of light brown sugar), 5 to 10 minutes. (Watch very carefully to avoid overcooking or you will get black flecks.) Remove from the heat at once and reserve until ready to use.

Fry the bacon in a medium (4- to 6-quart) cast-iron Dutch oven set over medium-high heat until crisp, 4 to 6 minutes. Remove bacon with a slotted spoon, leaving the drippings in the Dutch oven. Cool the bacon and crumble into a small bowl. Add the onion, garlic, celery, and bell peppers and cook, stirring often, until tender, 6 to 8 minutes.

Stir in the vegetable broth, reserved toasted flour, okra, corn, thyme, and cayenne until well blended. Bring to a boil.

Reduce the heat to low. Stir in the shrimp, tomatoes, vegetable juice, and parsley. Simmer, stirring, until the shrimp just turn pink and opaque, about 1 minute.

Working quickly, transfer the gumbo to a soup tureen. Stir in the filé-water mixture until well blended, and sprinkle with the reserved bacon. Serve over rice. Pass the red pepper sauce.

THAI-STYLE "PAELLA"

Makes 4 servings

SOME FRIENDS SERVED A CHINESE-STYLE paella at a dinner party and it inspired me to create this trans-ethnic version of the renowned Spanish paella. It hardly resembles the Spanish masterpiece except for a few of the exotic ingredients I have taken from it, but you'll find this different and exciting to the palate. I developed the recipe so that the empty headroom in the Dutch oven would naturally steam the rice and shrimp, which saves the cook several extra preparation steps compared to a typical rice-based dish.

2 tablespoons olive oil

1 medium yellow onion, minced

1 cup jasmine rice, cleaned and rinsed

½ teaspoon salt

1 teaspoon lightly packed saffron threads, soaked in 3 cups clam juice for 30 minutes

1 tablespoon finely chopped fresh lemongrass

1 pound medium shrimp, shelled and deveined

⅔ cup canned unsweetened coconut milk

1 cup fresh or thawed frozen green peas

¼ cup minced fresh parsley

Salt and freshly ground pepper, to taste

In a medium (4- to 6-quart) cast-iron Dutch oven over medium heat, heat the oil for 2 minutes. Add the onion and rice and cook, stirring frequently, until the onion is soft but not browned, 4 to 5 minutes.

Add the ½ teaspoon salt, saffron-clam juice mixture, and lemongrass and bring to a rolling boil, stirring occasionally. Reduce the heat to low, cover, and simmer until the rice is tender, about 20 minutes (do not stir). If after 20 minutes the rice isn't completely tender, stir in ½ cup water until well blended, cover, and cook for 10 minutes more, stirring occasionally.

Stir in the shrimp. Cover and let cook (do not lift the lid or stir) for 8 to 10 minutes more or until the shrimp is opaque and almost all the liquid has been absorbed.

Stir in the coconut milk, peas, and parsley until well blended, and season with salt and pepper. Transfer to a large serving platter, fluff with a fork, and serve at once.

COOKING IN CAST IRON

NOTE

Jasmine rice, coconut milk, and lemongrass are available in Thai markets, and gourmet stores. Bottled clam juice and saffron are available in gourmet stores and well-stocked supermarkets.

PASTA CAPONATA

CAPONATA IS A SICILIAN DISH that is generally served as a side dish, salad, or relish. Though I love it as a filling for a freshly baked Italian loaf, I find it makes a stupendous sauce for pasta. It is one of those dishes that benefits from being made a day or two in advance so the flavors have a chance to develop. Upon perusal of this recipe you may think that there is too much olive oil. But trust me, the extra-virgin olive oil is an essential part of the multi-dimensional flavor quality of the dish and provides a buttery quality to the cooked eggplant while enhancing the punch of the olives.

1 (1¾-ounce) jar pine nuts, called *pignoli* (about ½ cup), to garnish

¾ cup plus 2 tablespoons extra-virgin olive oil

1 medium eggplant (about 1¼ pounds), unpeeled and cut into ½-inch cubes

1 white onion, coarsely chopped

4 ribs celery, thinly sliced

1¼ pounds fresh plum tomatoes, coarsely chopped

½ teaspoon salt

½ cup red wine vinegar

2 tablespoons honey

1 (3½-ounce) jar capers, drained (about ½ cup)

1 cup whole pimiento-stuffed green olives

½ cup coarsely chopped pimiento-stuffed green olives

3 tablespoons minced fresh basil

Salt and freshly ground pepper, to taste

1 pound dry fettuccine pasta

Add the pine nuts to a medium (10- to 12-inch) cast-iron skillet over medium heat. Dry-toast the pine nuts, tossing, until golden brown, 5 to 7 minutes. Transfer them to a small bowl and reserve.

Return the skillet to medium heat and heat ½ cup of the oil for 2 minutes. Fry the eggplant in batches, stirring frequently, until lightly browned and tender but not falling apart, 8 to 10 minutes, adding up to another ¼ cup oil between each batch. Transfer the eggplant to a colander with a dish set underneath it to catch the oil and drain.

Meanwhile, return the skillet to medium heat, and heat the 2 tablespoons oil for 1 minute. Add the onion and celery and cook, stirring often, until the celery is crisp-tender, 5 to 7 minutes.

Stir in the tomatoes, salt, vinegar, honey, capers, and the whole and chopped olives. Cook, stirring often, for 20 minutes.

Stir in the drained eggplant and basil and season with salt and pepper.

MEANWHILE, PREPARE THE PASTA: Bring 3 quarts of water to a boil in a 6- to 8-quart pot over high heat. Stir in the pasta and return to a boil. Boil, stirring occasionally, until the pasta is al dente (slightly firm to the bite), 6 to 9 minutes. Drain the pasta in a colander. Transfer to a shallow serving bowl.

Ladle the sauce over the pasta and sprinkle with the reserved toasted pine nuts. Serve at once.

LINGUINE WITH WHITE CLAM SAUCE

Makes 4 to 6 servings

I'VE TAKEN LIBERTIES AND ADDED half-and-half, herbs, butter, and Parmesan cheese to this classic Italian pasta dish, and it always meets with rave reviews. Though this is a pleasingly, subtly flavored briny dish, the results of using canned chopped clams are, in effect, bland, and I don't recommend using them. This dish must be made with fresh clams. I have developed a method so the broth-like sauce is not in the skillet too long, otherwise there would be a risk of some of the sauce ingredients chemically reacting with the iron content of the skillet, resulting in a slight grayish cast to the sauce. Though not harmful, it isn't a pretty presentation. If your skillet is properly seasoned and you follow the directions there will be no problem. *Mangia bene!*

½ **cup water**

1 **cup dry white wine**

40 **manila or littleneck clams, scrubbed**

1 **pound dry linguine pasta**

3 **tablespoons extra-virgin olive oil**

4 **cloves garlic, crushed through a garlic press**

2 **cups bottled clam juice**

½ **cup half-and-half, at room temperature**

4 **tablespoons (½ stick) unsalted butter**

2 **tablespoons minced fresh basil**

1 **tablespoon minced fresh oregano**

Salt and freshly ground pepper, to taste

Freshly grated Parmesan cheese, to serve

Combine the water and ½ cup of the white wine in a pot large enough to accommodate the clams in a single layer, and set over high heat. Bring the liquid to a simmer. Add the clams and reduce the heat to medium-high. Cover the pot and steam the clams just until the shells open, 7 to 8 minutes, and remove the pot from the heat. Using a slotted spoon, transfer the clams to a bowl, being careful not to spill the liquid in the shells. Cover to keep warm until ready to serve. Discard any clams whose shells do not open.

MEANWHILE, PREPARE THE PASTA: Bring 3 quarts of water to a boil in a 6- to 8-quart pot over high heat. Stir in the pasta and return to a boil. Boil, stirring occasionally, until the pasta is al dente (slightly firm to the bite), 6 to 9 minutes.

While the clams are steaming and the pasta is cooking, heat the oil in a medium (10- to 12-inch) cast-iron skillet over medium heat for 1 minute. Add the garlic and cook for 1 minute, stirring.

Pour in the remaining ½ cup white wine (caution: mixture will splatter) and stir in the clam juice until well blended. Bring to a gentle simmer. Stir in the half-and-half, butter, basil, and oregano. Cook, stirring, just until the butter is melted, 1 minute, and season with salt and pepper.

Working quickly, drain the pasta and divide among 4 to 6 heated pasta bowls, pouring an equal amount of the sauce over each, and sprinkle with some Parmesan cheese. Arrange some of the clams around the pasta in each bowl, and serve at once.

SEARED SEA SCALLOP, SPINACH, AND STRAWBERRY SALAD WITH AMBROSIAL VINAIGRETTE

Makes 4 servings

THIS IS A VERY REFRESHING and satisfying supper salad that I make time and time again. You can add other complementary ingredients, too, for example, when in season, I also like to add a handful of pea shoots. If you don't have a kitchen garden from which to harvest these, they are now sold in farmers' markets and even some supermarkets.

DRESSING

¼ cup extra-virgin olive oil

¼ cup balsamic vinegar

2 tablespoons fresh lemon juice

3 tablespoons red currant jelly or preserves

¼ cup finely chopped fresh mint

Salt and freshly ground pepper, to taste

SALAD

1½ pounds fresh young spinach, stemmed and torn into bite-sized pieces, or mixed greens such as mesclun

2 pints fresh strawberries, hulled and thinly sliced

1 (7-ounce) log goat cheese, crumbled

2 (2.5-ounce) bags sliced almonds (1 cup total)

1 tablespoon olive oil

2 pounds sea scallops

Freshly ground pepper, to serve

TO MAKE THE DRESSING: Whisk together the oil, vinegar, lemon juice, jelly, and mint in a small bowl until well blended. Season to taste with the salt and pepper, and reserve until ready to use.

FOR THE SALAD: Line 4 dinner plates with the spinach. Sprinkle evenly with the strawberries, followed by the goat cheese, and set aside.

Place a large (12- to 14-inch) cast-iron skillet over medium heat and add the almonds. Dry-toast, stirring occasionally, until light golden brown, 5 to 7 minutes. Transfer to a heatproof bowl and reserve until ready to use.

Return the skillet to medium-high heat, add the oil, and heat for 1 minute. Add the scallops in a single layer and cook until golden brown and opaque throughout (no longer translucent), 4 to 6 minutes on each side.

Working quickly, top the salads with the warm scallops. Whisk the reserved dressing again to make sure it is still well blended and drizzle over all. Sprinkle each salad with the reserved almonds and a few grinds of the peppermill and serve at once.

LEMONGRASS-SCENTED SHRIMP WITH JASMINE RICE

Makes 4 servings

THIS FRAGRANT DISH HAS BIG flavor and takes relatively little time. Just start the jasmine rice ahead of time, begin this recipe during the last 10 minutes of the rice's cooking time, and they'll both be ready to serve at the same time.

3 tablespoons unsalted butter

1 pound medium shrimp, shelled, deveined

1 medium yellow onion, coarsely chopped

1 tablespoon curry powder

2 tablespoons thinly sliced fresh tender lemongrass (available at health food stores or Thai markets)

2 tablespoons freshly grated peeled fresh ginger

3 cloves garlic, crushed through a garlic press

1 teaspoon salt

½ teaspoon freshly ground pepper

1 (14-ounce) can unsweetened coconut milk (available at health food stores or Thai markets)

Juice of 1 medium lime

3 scallions, thinly sliced

¼ cup finely chopped fresh cilantro

Hot, cooked jasmine rice (available at health food stores or Thai markets)

Melt 1 tablespoon of the butter in a large (12- to 14-inch) cast-iron skillet over medium heat. Add the shrimp and cook, tossing, until they just turn pink and opaque, 4 to 5 minutes. Remove from the skillet and reserve.

Melt the remaining 2 tablespoons butter in the skillet. Add the onion, and cook, stirring occasionally, until translucent, 4 to 5 minutes.

Reduce the heat to low, and stir in the curry powder, lemongrass, ginger, garlic, salt, and pepper.

Add the coconut milk, lime juice, scallions, and cilantro, and stir until well blended. Add the reserved shrimp and taste, adding more salt and pepper if necessary. Cook, stirring constantly, until heated through, about 1 minute. Serve at once over the rice.

PASTA PUTTANESCA

THIS ROBUST SAUCE IS A famous pasta sauce from Italy, named a long time ago for ladies of the night. The Greek kalamata olives and the capers are available at gourmet stores and most supermarkets.

¼ cup extra-virgin olive oil

1 (2-ounce) can anchovy fillets

6 cloves garlic, crushed through a garlic press

2 (35-ounce cans) Italian plum tomatoes

1 (3.5-ounce) jar capers, drained

1½ cups pitted Greek kalamata olives, coarsely chopped

1½ cups pitted Greek kalamata olives, cut in half lengthwise

1 pound dry capellini pasta

¼ cup minced fresh oregano

Salt and freshly ground pepper, to taste

Freshly grated Parmesan, to serve

Combine the oil, anchovies, and garlic in a large (12- to 14-inch) cast iron skillet, and, using the back of a fork, mash thoroughly to form a paste. Place over medium heat.

Stir in the tomatoes, capers, and olives, breaking up the tomatoes using the back of a wooden spoon. Bring to a boil. Reduce the heat to medium-low and simmer for 1 hour, stirring occasionally.

Meanwhile, about 10 minutes before the sauce is ready, bring 3 quarts water to a boil in a 6- to 8-quart pot over high heat. Stir in the pasta and bring back to a boil. Boil, stirring occasionally, until the pasta is al dente (slightly firm to the bite), 4 to 6 minutes. Drain in a colander. Transfer pasta to a serving bowl.

Stir the oregano into the sauce, season with salt and pepper, and ladle over the pasta. Sprinkle with Parmesan cheese and serve at once.

SPAGHETTI PIE WITH PESTO AND VEGETABLE MEDLEY

Makes 4 servings

THIS TWIST ON LASAGNA USES the cast-iron skillet to create a lovely, crispy crust—and is a lot less time consuming.

> 2 tablespoons olive oil
>
> 1 pound dry spaghetti
>
> 3 cups (12 ounces) shredded mozzarella cheese
>
> 6 large eggs, beaten
>
> ¼ cup minced sun-dried tomatoes (available from gourmet shops and many supermarkets)
>
> 1 (16-ounce) package frozen vegetable medley, such as broccoli, cauliflower, and red bell peppers
>
> 1 (7-ounce) container basil pesto or ¾ cup homemade, at room temperature

Preheat the oven to 350F (175C). Grease a large (12- to 14-inch) cast iron skillet with the oil.

Bring 3 quarts of water to a boil in a 6- to 8-quart pot over high heat. Stir in the pasta and bring back to a boil. Boil, stirring occasionally, until al dente (slightly firm to the bite), 6 to 9 minutes. Drain and transfer to a large bowl.

Add the cheese, eggs, and tomatoes to the bowl and stir until well blended. Transfer to the prepared skillet, smooth the surface, and press down gently using a wooden spoon.

Bake for 30 minutes or until the spaghetti mixture is set.

During the last 10 minutes of baking time, cook the vegetable medley according to package directions.

Cut the pie into wedges and divide among the dinner plates. Using a slotted spoon, place the vegetables alongside the pie on each plate, ladle the pesto over all, and serve at once.

ITALIAN PASTA É FAGIOLI

Makes 4 to 6 servings

CREAMY-TEXTURED CANNELLINI BEANS ARE used in many Italian favorites, from entrée to side dish, even pureed as a topping for bruschetta. The delicately flavored cannellini beans carry the rich, fruity essence of extra-virgin olive oil well, which is another important component to this recipe and is drizzled on the soup at time of serving. The simplicity of this dish belies its strength. It is said that this pasta and bean soup originated in the Veneto region of Italy, but one version or another can be found all throughout Italy.

¼ cup extra-virgin olive oil, plus extra to serve

2 cloves garlic, crushed through a garlic press

1 cup minced yellow onion

2 cups finely diced carrots

2 cups finely diced celery

9 cups chicken stock or canned chicken broth

2 cups dry ditali (tube-shaped pasta) or other small, hollow pasta such as elbow-shaped macaroni

⅓ cup minced fresh basil

¼ cup minced fresh parsley

1 (19-ounce) can cannellini beans, drained and rinsed

Salt and freshly ground pepper, to taste

Freshly grated Parmesan cheese, to serve

Heat the ¼ cup oil in a medium (4- to 6-quart) cast-iron Dutch oven over medium heat for 1 minute. Add the garlic, onion, carrots, and celery and cook, stirring often, until the carrots are crisp-tender, 4 to 6 minutes.

Add the chicken stock and bring to a boil. Stir in the pasta and bring back to a boil. Boil, stirring occasionally, until the pasta is al dente (slightly firm to the bite) and the vegetables are tender, 4 to 6 minutes.

Stir in the basil, parsley, and beans until well blended. Cook, stirring occasionally, until the beans are heated through, 3 minutes more. Season to taste with salt and pepper.

Serve the soup in heated bowls with Parmesan cheese on the side, and pass a cruet of extra-virgin olive oil to drizzle over the soup.

BROCCOLI RABE WITH ORECCHIETTE, GARLIC, AND CRUSHED RED PEPPER

Makes 4 to 6 servings

I LOVE THE SCENT OF broccoli rabe. Once cooked, to me, it has an almost clover-like fragrance. It is now available at many supermarkets. You use the florets, leaves, and stems. In this recipe, the fruity extra-virgin olive oil, imbued with fresh garlic, becomes a perfumed light "sauce" for the orecchiette pasta, which entraps the broccoli rabe florets.

1 pound broccoli rabe, stems trimmed to an even 3-inch length

½ cup extra-virgin olive oil

5 cloves garlic, crushed through a garlic press

1 pound dry orecchiette (little ears pasta), cooked according to package directions, drained, and brought to room temperature

½ cup freshly grated Romano cheese, or to taste

Salt, to taste

½ teaspoon dried red pepper flakes, or to taste

Bring 2 quarts water to a boil in a 4- to 6-quart saucepan over medium heat. Add the broccoli rabe and bring to a boil. Boil until tender, 5 to 8 minutes, and drain. Reserve until ready to use.

Heat the oil in a large (12- to 14-inch) cast-iron skillet over medium heat for 1 minute. Add the garlic and cook for 1 minute. Add the reserved broccoli rabe and cooked orecchiette and stir until well blended. (If the broccoli rabe leaves clump together, separate them with a fork.)

Transfer to a warm serving bowl. Sprinkle with the Romano cheese, and season to taste with salt, dried red pepper flakes, and more Romano cheese, if desired. Serve at once.

SIDE DISHES

Algerian Carrot Salad

Roasted Asparagus with Parmesan-Ricotta

Cowboy Beans

Gingered Stewed Beets

Colcannon

Eggplant with Sun-Dried Tomatoes

Endive with Lemon

Chinese-American Fried Rice

Spanish Stewed Garbanzo Beans

"Just-Right" Grits

Israel-Style Roasted Root Vegetables with Za' atar

Jerusalem Artichoke Sauté

Jewish-American Potato Latkes

Old-Fashioned Macaroni and Cheese

Maquechoux

Mexican Rice with Annatto and Avocado

Indian Basmati Pilau

Polenta Parmesan

Warm Wild-Mushroom Salad

Pomegranate-Glazed Radicchio

Rosemary Potato Wedges

Red Beans and Rice

Roasted Red Pepper-Gorgonzola Bread Pudding

Asian-Style Roasted Peanut Pasta Salad with Cilantro

Zucchini Romano

Scalloped Potatoes

Succotash

ALGERIAN CARROT SALAD

Makes 4 to 6 servings

I HAVE ADDED WALNUT OIL as a base to this Algerian-inspired carrot salad.

2 pounds carrots, thinly sliced

¼ cup plus 2 tablespoons walnut oil (available from supermarkets or gourmet shops)

1 medium yellow onion, finely chopped

3 cloves garlic, crushed through a garlic press

3 tablespoons fresh lemon juice

1 tablespoon firmly packed light brown sugar

1 tablespoon ground cumin

⅛ teaspoon ground cayenne pepper

⅛ cup minced fresh cilantro

⅛ cup minced fresh parsley

1 cup pitted dates (4 ounces), finely chopped

Salt and freshly ground pepper, to taste

Add the carrots and enough water to cover by 2 inches to a 2- to 3-quart saucepan and bring to a boil over medium-high heat.

Reduce heat to low and simmer until tender, about 8 minutes. Drain and reserve until ready to use.

Heat the 2 tablespoons of oil in a large (12- to 14-inch) cast-iron skillet over medium heat. Add the onion and garlic and cook, stirring, until the onion is tender, 4 minutes. Add the reserved carrots and cook for 2 minutes more, stirring often.

Meanwhile, prepare the dressing in a small bowl: Whisk together the ¼ cup oil, lemon juice, brown sugar, cumin, cayenne, cilantro, and parsley until well blended.

Combine the carrot mixture, dressing, and dates in a serving bowl, and toss until well blended. Season with salt and pepper. Serve at once or let cool to room temperature and serve.

ROASTED ASPARAGUS WITH PARMESAN-RICOTTA

Makes 4 to 6 servings

ENDEARINGLY SIMPLE AND AN IDEAL candidate to accompany a leisurely supper, roasting truly pulls out the flavor of the asparagus. Medium-thick rather than pencil-thin asparagus work best for roasting. For variation, garnish with freshly grated lemon zest in place of the Parmesan-ricotta mixture.

> **3 pounds medium asparagus (Choose asparagus as close as possible to one another in size and thickness.)**
>
> **1 (15-ounce) container ricotta cheese**
>
> **½ cup freshly grated Parmesan cheese**
>
> **½ teaspoon salt**
>
> **¾ teaspoon freshly ground pepper**
>
> **4 tablespoons (½ stick) unsalted butter**

Snap the tough ends from the asparagus spears and use only the tender tips for this recipe. (The asparagus spears will snap off naturally where they become tough if you hold both ends and bend the spear; see Cook's Tip below.)

Bring 3 quarts of water to a boil in a 6- to 8-quart pot over medium-high heat. Add the asparagus tips and cook until tender (but not limp) when pierced with a fork, 4 to 6 minutes. Drain well (any excess water will dilute the flavor of the topping) and set aside to cool briefly.

Meanwhile, while the asparagus is cooking, combine the ricotta, Parmesan cheese, salt, and pepper in a medium bowl and stir until well blended. Reserve at room temperature until ready to use.

Preheat the broiler. Liberally grease the interior of a large (12- to 14-inch) cast-iron skillet with 1 tablespoon of the butter. Add the asparagus in a single layer. Cut the remaining 3 tablespoons of butter into small bits and dot the asparagus with the butter.

Slide the skillet under the broiler 4 to 6 inches from the heat source and broil for 5 to 8 minutes or until the asparagus is dappled golden brown all over; use a fork to rotate the asparagus every 2 to 3 minutes. (Watch the asparagus carefully so it does not burn.)

Top with the ricotta mixture and serve at once directly from the skillet.

COOK'S TIP

There is a wonderful use for the tough ends of asparagus that are usually discarded: Boil them until tender, then drain. Purée and strain, then stir in melted butter to taste for asparagus purée.

COWBOY BEANS

THIS IS A VERY SIMPLE, basic dish; the kind I put in the "campfire cuisine" category. It is carefully seasoned so that you can still taste the beans, but because pinto beans can carry a lot of flavor, feel free to create an altogether new dish by adding some of your own seasonings.

Salt pork is salt-cured pork fat (usually with some streaks of lean). When tightly wrapped, it can be stored in the refrigerator for up to a month.

> **1 pound dried pinto or navy beans, picked over**
>
> **2 tablespoons olive oil**
>
> **2 medium yellow onions, coarsely chopped**
>
> **4 ounces salt pork, finely diced, or 6 slices bacon, diced**
>
> **1½ cups barbecue sauce**
>
> **⅓ cup ketchup**
>
> **2 teaspoons celery salt**
>
> **Salt and freshly ground pepper, to taste**
>
> **Hot red pepper sauce, to serve**

Soak the pinto beans overnight in cold water to cover by 2 inches, covered, at room temperature. Drain and rinse.

Heat the oil in a medium (4- to 6-quart) cast-iron Dutch oven over medium-high heat for 1 minute. Stir in the onions and cook, stirring, until the onion is soft but not browned, 3 minutes.

Add the beans, salt pork, and enough cold water to cover by 3 inches. Bring to a boil, then reduce the heat to low and simmer, stirring occasionally, until the beans are very tender but still hold their shape, 2 to 4 hours.

Stir in the barbecue sauce, ketchup, and celery salt until well blended. Season with salt and pepper.

To serve, transfer to a warm soup tureen or individual soup bowls and pass with the hot red pepper sauce.

GINGERED STEWED BEETS

Makes 4 to 6 servings

YOU CAN USE FRESH BEETS from your garden, cooked and sliced for this recipe. However, to save time, and so the recipe can be prepared year-round, I call for canned beets, which are an excellent product.

> **6 tablespoons unsalted butter**
>
> **2 tablespoons all-purpose flour**
>
> **¼ cup firmly packed light brown sugar**
>
> **2 (15-ounce) cans sliced beets, strained, reserving the beet juice**
>
> **1 teaspoon ground ginger**
>
> **Salt and freshly ground pepper, to taste**

In a medium (10- to 12-inch) cast-iron skillet over medium heat, melt the butter. Add the flour and brown sugar and whisk until well blended and smooth. Whisk in all of the beet juice and bring to a boil to thicken the sauce.

Reduce the heat to low and whisk in the ginger until well blended. Gently stir in the beets (so as not to break them) and cook just until heated through, 3 minutes. Season with salt and pepper and serve at once.

COLCANNON

I AM SO INFATUATED WITH this Irish dish (sometimes made with kale in place of cabbage) that I have even eaten it cold.

¼ cup olive oil

1 cup finely chopped yellow onion

4 cups loosely packed finely shredded Savoy or green cabbage (about ¾ pound)

5 cups firmly packed smooth mashed cooked potatoes, seasoned to taste with melted butter

3 tablespoons strong coarse mustard

Salt and freshly ground pepper, to taste

Heat the oil in a large (12- to 14-inch) cast-iron skillet over medium heat for 2 minutes. Add the onion and cabbage and cook, stirring often, until the onion and cabbage are lightly browned, 8 to 10 minutes.

Stir in the mashed potatoes and mustard until well blended. Cook, stirring, just until the mashed potatoes are heated through, about 1 minute. Season with salt and pepper and serve at once.

Eggplant with Sun-Dried Tomatoes

Makes 4 to 6 servings

THE ZESTY SUN-DRIED TOMATOES add interest and charm to the ubiquitous, meaty eggplant of this side dish.

3 tablespoons extra-virgin olive oil

2 medium eggplant (2 pounds total), unpeeled, trimmed, and cut crosswise into ½-inch-thick slices, then cut into ½-inch cubes

½ cup water

¼ cup minced sun-dried tomatoes (available from many supermarkets or gourmet stores)

4 cloves garlic, crushed through a garlic press

2 tablespoons minced fresh oregano

½ teaspoon salt

½ teaspoon freshly ground pepper

Heat the oil in a large (12- to 14-inch) cast-iron skillet over medium-high heat for 1 minute. Add the eggplant and sauté for 2 minutes.

Stir in the water until well blended. Cover and cook, stirring often, until the eggplant is tender, 10 to 15 minutes. Stir in the remaining ingredients until well blended and serve.

ENDIVE WITH LEMON

Makes 4 servings

BELGIAN ENDIVE IS A SMALL (about 6-inch-long), cigar-shaped head of tightly-packed, cream-colored faintly-bitter leaves; it's grown in complete darkness to prevent the leaves from turning green. It is available in American supermarkets from September through May.

To prepare endives, trim off ⅛ inch from the root end of each. Once cooked, endive has a very different flavor than when raw.

2 tablespoons plus 2 teaspoons extra-virgin olive oil

4 Belgian endives (¾ to 1 pound total), do not core

1 cup water

2 tablespoons unsalted butter, melted

2 tablespoons fresh lemon juice

Salt and freshly ground pepper, to taste

Preheat the oven to 425F (220C). Grease the interior of a medium (10- to 12-inch) cast-iron skillet with the 2 teaspoons oil.

Arrange the endives in a single layer in the prepared skillet. Drizzle evenly with the 2 tablespoons oil and add the water. Roast for 3 to 6 minutes, or until when pierced with a fork in the thickest part, the tines just go through without too much resistance.

Using tongs, transfer the endives to a serving plate (drain off any cooking liquid). Drizzle with the melted butter, followed by the lemon juice. Season with salt and pepper and serve at once.

CHINESE-AMERICAN FRIED RICE

Makes 4 to 6 servings

THIS DISH IS EXTREMELY TEXTURALLY satisfying and scrumptious.

3 tablespoons peanut oil

1 medium white onion, minced

3 cloves garlic, crushed through a garlic press

3 tablespoons minced peeled fresh ginger

2 cups cooked regular long-grain rice

2½ tablespoons soy sauce

2 tablespoons dark sesame oil

¼ cup dry sherry

4 scallions, white and green parts, thinly sliced on the diagonal

3 large eggs, beaten

Salt and freshly ground pepper, to taste

Add the oil to a cast-iron wok, rotating the wok to coat the sides, and heat over medium heat until the oil is rippling, about 1 minute.

Add the onion, garlic, and ginger and stir-fry until the mixture is aromatic but not browned, about 1 second.

Add the cooked rice, soy sauce, sesame oil, and Sherry and stir-fry for 2 minutes, breaking up any lumps of grains and blend the mixture well. Stir in the scallions and stir-fry, tossing quickly but gently for 10 seconds.

Pour the eggs into the center of the wok and immediately stir to combine, tossing the eggs with the rice until the eggs have scrambled lightly and are broken up into small pieces, about 1 minute. (Watch carefully and do not overcook or the eggs will become dry.) Season with salt and pepper. Transfer to a serving dish and serve at once.

SPANISH STEWED GARBANZO BEANS

Makes 4 servings

THIS SIDE DISH MAKES THE most of the ever-popular garbanzo bean. It is as pretty as it is tasty.

3 tablespoons extra-virgin olive oil

3 cloves garlic, crushed through a garlic press

13 ounces fresh spinach, stemmed and leaves torn into bite-sized pieces

1 medium tomato, peeled, seeded, and minced

1 teaspoon lightly packed saffron threads (available from gourmet shops and many supermarkets)

1 teaspoon salt

¼ teaspoon freshly ground pepper

2 (15½-ounce cans) garbanzo beans (chickpeas), drained and rinsed

Heat the oil in a large (12- to 14-inch) cast-iron skillet over medium heat for 1 minute. Add the garlic, spinach, tomato, saffron, salt, and pepper. Cook, stirring, just until the spinach has wilted and is tender, 3 minutes. (It may seem as if there is too much spinach for the size of skillet, but the spinach will cook down rapidly.)

Stir in the garbanzo beans and cook, stirring, just until the garbanzo beans are heated through, about 2 minutes, and serve.

"JUST-RIGHT" GRITS

Makes 4 servings

TO ME "JUST RIGHT" IS when the grits are slightly soupy but thick enough that they do not run off the plate when served. You can mail-order whole-grain grits from The Nora Mill Granary. Tel. # 1-800-927-2375 or http://www.noramill.com.

- 2 tablespoons bacon drippings or unsalted butter
- 2 cups water
- 1 cup whole-grain (not instant) grits
- 2 cups half-and-half, or more, as needed for desired consistency
- Salt and freshly ground pepper, to taste

Heat the bacon drippings in a medium (10- to 12-inch) cast-iron skillet over medium heat. Stir in the water and bring to a boil.

Stir in the grits and return to a boil. Reduce the heat to low, and stir in the half-and-half until well blended and the mixture is smooth. Simmer for 15 minutes, stirring often. Add more half-and-half if needed for desired consistency. Season with salt and pepper, and serve at once.

ISRAEL-STYLE ROASTED ROOT VEGETABLES WITH ZA' ATAR

Makes 4 to 6 servings

THIS RECIPE IS ADAPTED FROM the "Roasted Carrot and Feta Salad with Za' atar" recipe in Todd English's and Sally Sampson's *The Figs Table*. In one word, this recipe is superb. Za' atar seasoning blend is available from Penzeys Spices. Tel. # 1-800-741-7787 or http://www.penzeys.com. Both roasted red peppers and Greek kalamata olives are available at gourmet stores and most supermarkets.

1½ pounds carrots, cut into ½-inch cubes

½ pound baking potatoes, cut into ½-inch cubes

½ pound parsnips, cut into ½-inch cubes

3 tablespoons olive oil

1 teaspoon salt

¼ teaspoon freshly ground pepper

1 (12-ounce) jar roasted red peppers, drained and cut into ¼-inch-wide strips (about 1¼ cups total)

½ cup pitted Greek kalamata olives, cut in half lengthwise

2½ tablespoons za' atar seasoning blend

8 ounces feta cheese, crumbled

Preheat the oven to 400F (205C). Stir together the carrots, potatoes, parsnips, oil, salt, and pepper in a large (12- to 14-inch) cast-iron skillet. Bake for 50 minutes, stirring occasionally, or until the vegetables test very tender when pierced with a fork.

Transfer the roasted vegetables to a medium serving bowl along with all the remaining ingredients except for the feta cheese and stir until well blended. Top with the feta cheese and serve at once.

JERUSALEM ARTICHOKE SAUTÉ

Makes 4 servings

JERUSALEM ARTICHOKES ARE THE TUBER of a variety of sunflower, also called Sunchokes. They are available in the produce section of many markets, usually in the fall and winter. Once cooked, I find the flavor is rich, with the taste of sunflower seeds but the texture of a potato. To prepare, simply scrub them clean. Once cut into, they discolor quickly, so have all your other recipe ingredients prepped so you are ready to cook!

½ to ⅔ cup olive oil

1 pound Jerusalem artichokes, cut into ¼-inch-thick slices

4 tablespoons (½ stick) unsalted butter, melted

2 tablespoons fresh lemon juice

⅛ cup minced fresh parsley

⅓ cup salted sunflower seeds

Salt and freshly ground pepper, to taste

Heat the oil in a large (12- to 14-inch) cast-iron skillet over medium-high heat for 2 minutes. Add the Jerusalem artichokes and cook, stirring occasionally, until golden brown and fork-tender, 9 to 12 minutes.

Using a slotted spoon, transfer the Jerusalem artichokes to a paper towel-lined plate to drain. Transfer to a serving bowl and toss with the butter, lemon juice, parsley, and sunflower seeds until well coated. Season with salt and pepper, and serve at once.

Jewish-American Potato Latkes

IN THIS RECIPE FOR LATKES (grated potato pancakes), I have made a departure from the norm and added grated carrots. In addition, I like to keep the skin on the potatoes when I grate them, because so many nutrients are contained in the skin and because it doesn't affect the presentation since they are pan-fried and have a light brown crust anyway.

2 pounds baking potatoes, unpeeled

1 medium white onion

2 medium carrots

1 large egg, beaten

1 tablespoon minced fresh parsley

½ teaspoon salt

3 tablespoons matzo meal (available from supermarkets or Jewish grocery stores)

¼ teaspoon baking powder

¾ to 1 cup vegetable oil, to fry

Applesauce, to serve

Shred the potatoes, onion, and carrots into long, thin strips, using the shredding disk of a food processor or the large holes of a 4-sided box grater. As you shred, transfer the vegetables to a large colander. Using your hands, squeeze the mixture to release any excess moisture.

Transfer the potato mixture to a large bowl; add the egg, parsley, salt, matzo meal, and baking powder and stir until well blended.

Preheat oven to 200F (95C). Add the oil to a depth of ¼ inch in a large (12- to 14-inch) cast-iron skillet. Heat over medium heat until the oil sputters, about 3 minutes.

Working quickly, drop loosely packed ⅓ cupfuls of the mixture into the skillet and, using a spatula, flatten each into a cake 4 inches in diameter. Fry the potato cakes in batches, making sure the edges do not overlap, until the exterior is golden brown and crispy, 3 to 4 minutes on each side. Add up to ¼ cup more oil as needed to maintain the depth of ¼ inch, and reheat the oil between batches.

Drain the latkes on a paper towel-lined baking sheet between batches, then discard the paper towels and transfer the baking sheet with latkes to the warm oven and hold until ready to serve. Serve at once and pass applesauce alongside.

OLD-FASHIONED MACARONI AND CHEESE

I AM HAUNTED BY the fact that for years I have been chasing the best old-fashioned macaroni and cheese recipe. I have tried every imaginable cheese known to man (and mouse), and then some. I even used to work in a cheese shop. Finally, after many tests, I've got it. I think this recipe, using a blend of cheeses, is the best old-fashioned mac 'n' cheese I have ever had. (I should know; I live in the South, where mac 'n' cheese is considered a vegetable!)

3 tablespoons unsalted butter

2 tablespoons all-purpose flour

1½ teaspoons salt

¼ teaspoon freshly ground pepper

2 cups milk

6 to 7 ounces elbow macaroni (about 2 cups)

3 cups shredded cheese (about ¾ pound); choose a blend of Monterey Jack, cheddar, and American cheese

Salt and freshly ground pepper, to taste

Preheat the oven to 375F (190C). To make the sauce: Melt 2 tablespoons of the butter in a 2- to 3-quart saucepan over medium heat. Whisk in the flour, ½ teaspoon of the salt, and pepper until smooth. Remove the pan from the heat and pour in the milk. Return the saucepan to medium heat and bring to a boil. Boil for 1 minute, whisking constantly. Remove the saucepan from the heat and reserve until ready to use.

Meanwhile, bring 3 quarts of water and the 1 teaspoon salt to boil in a 6- to 8-quart pot over high heat. Stir in the macaroni and return to a boil. Boil, stirring occasionally, until al dente (slightly firm to the bite), 3 to 5 minutes.

Drain the macaroni and transfer to a medium (10- to 12-inch) cast-iron skillet. Pour the sauce over the macaroni. Add the cheese and stir until the macaroni is well coated. Season to taste with salt and pepper. Smooth the surface and dot evenly with the remaining 1 tablespoon butter.

Cover the skillet with a lid and bake for 30 minutes on the middle rack of the oven. Uncover and bake for 15 minutes more or until the cheese has melted, the dish is bubbly, and the edges golden brown. Serve directly from the skillet.

SIDE DISHES

MAQUECHOUX

Makes 4 to 6 servings

ALSO KNOWN AS "MOCK SHOE" and "mark show," maquechoux means "false cabbage." No one seems to know why, as this Cajun dish has nothing to do with the texture of cabbage.

5 strips bacon

1 medium yellow onion, finely chopped

1 large green bell pepper, finely chopped

2 medium tomatoes, seeded and finely chopped

1 teaspoon sugar

2 cups fresh corn kernels or 1 (9-ounce) package frozen corn kernels, thawed

½ cup heavy cream, at room temperature

Salt and freshly ground pepper, to taste

Hot pepper sauce, to serve

Add the bacon to a medium (10- to 12-inch) cast-iron skillet over medium heat and fry until crisp, 4 to 6 minutes. Using tongs, transfer the bacon, leaving the dripping in the skillet, to paper towels. Crumble the bacon and reserve until ready to use.

Place the skillet with the bacon drippings over medium heat and heat for 1 minute. Add the onion and bell pepper and cook, stirring occasionally, until the bell pepper is tender, 5 minutes. Stir in the tomatoes and sugar and cook for 3 minutes, stirring occasionally.

Stir in the corn and cream, and cook, stirring constantly, until the corn is heated through, 4 minutes. Season with salt and pepper and sprinkle with the reserved crumbled bacon. Serve at once and pass with the hot pepper sauce.

MEXICAN RICE WITH ANNATTO AND AVOCADO

Makes 4 to 6 servings

MY VERSION OF MEXICAN RICE uses annatto, which gives it a reddish-orange cast, a lovely complement to the other colors in the dish. Since annatto can be difficult to find nationwide, I have called for the "Coriander and Annatto seasoning blend" made by the Goya Company that is generally available in most supermarkets.

2 tablespoons olive oil

1 cup long-grain white rice

3 cloves garlic, crushed through a garlic press

1¾ cups canned chicken broth

1 tablespoon coriander and annatto seasoning blend

1 cup fresh or thawed frozen green peas

1 medium avocado, to garnish

2 tablespoons fresh lime juice

½ cup firmly packed fresh cilantro leaves

Salt and freshly ground pepper, to taste

Heat the oil in a medium (4- to 6-quart) cast-iron Dutch oven over medium heat for 1 minute. Stir in the rice and garlic until well coated with the oil. Cook, stirring, for 2 minutes.

Stir in the chicken broth and seasoning blend and bring to a boil. Reduce the heat to low and cover. Simmer, stirring once, until the rice is tender and almost all the liquid is absorbed, 15 to 20 minutes.

Remove the Dutch oven from the heat. Add the peas, but do not stir (the steam will cook them gently so that they will remain bright green). Cover and let stand for 5 minutes more.

Meanwhile, peel, pit, and thinly slice the avocado lengthwise.

Stir the lime juice and cilantro into the rice mixture. Season to taste with salt and pepper and serve at once, garnished with the avocado slices.

INDIAN BASMATI PILAU

Makes 6 to 8 servings

TO SAVE TIME AND EFFORT, yet still offer a mix of vegetables to this aromatic pilau, I have called for two different mixtures of frozen mixed vegetable medleys (available in the grocer's freezer).

2 tablespoons olive oil

1 medium yellow onion, minced

2 medium cloves garlic, minced

3 tablespoons unsalted butter

2 tablespoons freshly grated peeled ginger

1½ tablespoons curry powder

¼ teaspoon ground cinnamon

¼ teaspoon ground ginger

¼ teaspoon ground cloves

½ teaspoon freshly ground pepper

2 cups basmati rice (available at Indian markets)

4½ cups canned vegetable broth

1 cup dry white wine

1 lightly packed teaspoon saffron threads (available from gourmet stores or supermarkets)

1 teaspoon salt

2 (16-ounce) packages frozen mixed vegetable medley (use 2 different blends, such as carrots, green beans, and yellow wax beans, plus another one), thawed

1 cup dried zante currants (available at health food stores or supermarkets) or raisins

1 cup salted cashews, coarsely chopped

Salt and freshly ground pepper, to taste

In a medium (4- to 6-quart) cast-iron Dutch oven, heat the oil over medium heat for 1 minute. Add the onion, garlic, butter, fresh ginger, curry powder, cinnamon, ground ginger, cloves, and pepper.

Cook, stirring, for 1 minute to allow the spices to lightly toast and release their aroma.

Add the rice and cook, stirring constantly, for 4 minutes. Stir in the broth, wine, saffron, salt, and vegetables.

Cover and cook the rice mixture without lifting the lid or stirring until the rice is just tender but not mushy, 15 to 20 minutes.

Remove the Dutch oven from the heat and add the currants and chopped cashews. Using a fork, gently toss until well blended. Season with salt and pepper and serve at once.

POLENTA PARMESAN

Makes 4 to 6 servings

A STAPLE OF NORTHERN ITALY, polenta is very versatile fare. Here I have graced it with a refreshing fresh basil-spiked tomato topping, which makes for an ample appetizer, especially when sprinkled with the rich flavor of some tangy Parmesan cheese.

POLENTA

2 teaspoons butter, to grease

4 cups water

1½ teaspoons salt

1½ cups yellow cornmeal, mixed with ½ cup cold water until well blended (to help prevent lumping)

TOPPING

3 medium tomatoes, seeded and diced

¼ cup finely chopped fresh basil

Salt and freshly ground pepper, to taste

4 tablespoons olive oil

½ cup freshly grated Parmesan cheese, to serve

TO PREPARE THE POLENTA: Lightly grease a 13 × 9-inch baking dish with the butter.

In a heavy 6- to 8-quart pot over medium-high heat, bring the 4 cups water and the salt to a boil. Reduce the heat to low and gradually add the cornmeal-water mixture, pouring in a thin, steady stream while whisking vigorously.

Cook, stirring frequently, until the polenta is smooth (no lumps), very thick, and pulls away from the sides of the pan, 5 minutes. Working quickly, transfer to the prepared baking dish. Using a spatula, pack down firmly and smooth the top. Reserve at room temperature until ready to use. When firm, cut in half lengthwise, then crosswise into 1-inch-wide strips.

TO MAKE THE TOPPING: Combine the tomatoes and basil in a medium bowl. Season with salt and pepper. Cover and set aside at room temperature until ready to serve.

Preheat the oven to 200F (95C). Heat 2 tablespoons of the olive oil in a large (12- to 14-inch) cast-iron skillet for 2 minutes. Add half of the polenta strips and cook until golden brown, 2 to

3 minutes on each side. Drain on a paper towel-lined plate, then transfer to a baking sheet and hold in the warm oven until ready to serve. Repeat with the remaining polenta and oil.

Divide the polenta strips among the dinner plates, divide the topping over the polenta, sprinkle with the Parmesan cheese, and serve at once.

WARM WILD-MUSHROOM SALAD

Makes 4 servings

I AM PLEASED THAT, DUE to high demand, wild mushrooms are now making their way into many American supermarkets. This side dish (or appetizer) goes together quickly and is choice autumnal or winter fare.

12 leaves Boston lettuce

¼ pound Parmesan cheese

4 tablespoons extra-virgin olive oil

¾ pound assorted wild mushrooms, such as porcini, oyster, and cremini, stemmed and very thinly sliced

Salt and freshly ground pepper, to taste

Line 4 salad plates with the lettuce leaves. Using a cheese planer/slicer, shave the cheese into sheets onto a piece of waxed paper and reserve until ready to use.

Heat 2 tablespoons of the oil in a medium (10- to 12-inch) cast-iron skillet over medium-high heat for 1 minute. Add the mushrooms and cook, tossing, until the mushrooms are fork-tender, 8 to 10 minutes.

Using a slotted spoon, place a mound of the mushrooms on each of the prepared plates. Working quickly, place some of the sheets of cheese over each. Season with salt and pepper, drizzle with some of the remaining 2 tablespoons oil, and serve at once.

POMEGRANATE-GLAZED RADICCHIO

Makes 4 servings

BECAUSE OF ITS BITTER FLAVOR, the burgundy-red-leafed-with-white-ribs radicchio di Verona now seen in our supermarkets is an acquired taste. This particular variety of Italian chicory is often used as a salad green. Here I have allied radicchio with pomegranate molasses, which bestows a sweet-tart extraordinary depth of flavor to the dish. I forecast culinary trends very carefully, and I believe that, though rarely used now, in the coming years pomegranate molasses, along with some others such as fig molasses, will be as readily used in the American kitchen as balsamic vinegar is now. For the final dish, you can expect the roasted raddichio to take on a chestnut brown color.

> 2 tablespoons plus 2 teaspoons extra-virgin olive oil
>
> 2 medium heads radicchio (¾ pound total), cut into quarters (do not core)
>
> ⅛ cup pomegranate molasses (available at gourmet and Middle Eastern markets)
>
> Salt and freshly ground pepper, to taste

Preheat the oven to 425F (220C). Grease a medium (10- to 12-inch) cast-iron skillet with the 2 teaspoons oil.

Arrange the radicchio wedges in a single layer on their sides in the prepared skillet. Drizzle evenly with the 2 tablespoons oil. Roast for 3 minutes.

Using tongs, turn the wedges over and roast for 3 to 5 minutes more or until when pierced in the thickest part with a fork, the tines just go through without too much resistance. Transfer to a serving plate, drizzle with the pomegranate molasses, season with salt and pepper, and serve at once.

ROSEMARY POTATO WEDGES

THE HUMBLE POTATO IS ELEVATED to new heights with this simple preparation that will stoke your palate and keep you coming back for more!

6 strips bacon

½ cup finely chopped onion

2 pounds baking potatoes, each potato peeled, cooked, and cut into 8 wedges

2 tablespoons minced fresh rosemary

½ teaspoon salt, or to taste

¼ teaspoon freshly ground pepper

Cook the bacon in a large (12- to 14-inch) cast-iron skillet over medium heat until crisp, 4 to 6 minutes. Using tongs, transfer the bacon to paper towels, leaving the dripping in the skillet. Crumble the bacon and reserve until ready to use.

Set the skillet with the bacon drippings over medium heat, add the onion, and cook, stirring occasionally, until tender, 3 minutes.

Reduce the heat to medium and stir in the remaining ingredients. Cook, stirring occasionally, until the potatoes are light golden brown, about 6 minutes. (If you want them even browner, place the skillet 4 to 6 inches under a preheated broiler for 10 to 15 seconds, watching closely so the potatoes do not burn.) Sprinkle with the reserved bacon and serve at once.

RED BEANS AND RICE

Makes 4 to 6 servings

I DID NOT INCLUDE SMOKED ham in my streamlined version of this celebrated Louisiana favorite so vegetarians can relish it, too. However, for you meat-eaters, if there is any leftover, it is also wonderful mixed with leftover chili. Here's a little trivia from *The Food Lover's Companion* by Sharon Tyler Herbst: "This dish was purportedly so loved by the famous trumpeter Louis Armstrong that he used to sign his personal letters 'Red beans and ricely yours.' "

2 teaspoons olive oil

3 cloves garlic, crushed through a garlic press

1 medium yellow onion, minced

1 cup minced celery

1 cup regular long-grain rice

2 cups canned vegetable broth

1 (15.5-ounce) can red kidney beans, drained and rinsed

1 large tomato, coarsely chopped

1 teaspoon ground cumin

3 scallions, green part only, thinly sliced

¼ to ¾ cup water

Salt and freshly ground pepper, to taste

Hot pepper sauce, to serve

Heat the oil in a large (12- to 14-inch) cast-iron skillet over medium heat for 1 minute. Add the garlic, onion, and celery and cook, stirring often, until the onion is tender, 6 minutes.

Stir in the rice and vegetable broth until well blended. Reduce the heat to medium-low, cover, and simmer, stirring occasionally, until the rice is tender, 20 minutes. (Add up to ½ cup water if necessary to prevent rice from sticking to skillet.)

Stir in the beans, tomato, cumin, scallions, and ¼ cup water until well blended. Cook, uncovered, just until the beans are heated through, stirring, 5 minutes. Season with salt and pepper. Serve at once, and pass the hot pepper sauce.

ROASTED RED PEPPER-GORGONZOLA BREAD PUDDING

Makes 4 to 6 servings

I AM ALWAYS ON THE lookout for unusual side dishes for brunch, and they seem a rarity. So one day I created this light-textured but robust savory bread pudding. The pungent Gorgonzola is an intense contrast to the vegetal roasted red peppers. I have made it with a multi-grain bread, potato bread, or an olive-walnut bread from the bakery. However, you can use any fresh bread or day-old leftover bread as long as it is not sweet.

1 teaspoon unsalted butter, to grease

1½ cups milk

1 cup heavy cream

6 large egg yolks

2 large eggs

½ cup sour cream

3 tablespoons minced fresh basil

1 (12-ounce jar) roasted red peppers, drained and coarsely chopped (1 cup)

1 teaspoon salt

½ teaspoon freshly ground black pepper

¾ pound loaf bread of your choice (but not a sweet bread), cut into ½-inch cubes

4½ ounces Gorgonzola cheese or other blue cheese, crumbled (1 cup)

Preheat the oven to 325F (165C). Grease a medium (10- to 12-inch) cast-iron skillet with the butter.

In a medium saucepan over medium heat, heat the milk and cream, stirring often, just until it comes to a boil. Meanwhile, in a medium heatproof bowl, whisk the egg yolks, eggs, and sour cream until well blended.

Gradually whisk the hot milk mixture into the egg mixture until well blended. Strain into another heatproof bowl and stir in 2 tablespoons of the basil, the roasted red peppers, salt, and pepper.

Evenly spread half of the bread cubes in the prepared skillet. Cover with half of the milk mixture and sprinkle with half of the Gorgonzola. Top with the remaining bread cubes, then the remaining milk mixture, and finally the remaining Gorgonzola. Run a knife around the inside of the skillet to help the milk-egg mixture run under the bread.

Bake on the middle rack of the oven for 50 to 60 minutes, or until a knife inserted 1 inch from the center of the pudding comes out almost clean with a few moist crumbs (not wet batter) clinging to it.

Let stand for 10 minutes before serving. Sprinkle evenly with the remaining 1 tablespoon basil and serve directly from the skillet.

ASIAN-STYLE ROASTED PEANUT PASTA SALAD WITH CILANTRO

THIS SPICY TANGLE OF PASTA makes a marvelous side dish for four or appetizer for six. Or double it and toss in some shredded cooked pork or chicken for a main course. Another one of the many virtues of cast iron is that it works wonderfully to dry-toast nuts, as illustrated in this recipe.

> **8 ounces dry fettuccine**
>
> **3 tablespoons sesame oil**
>
> **⅔ cup peanuts**
>
> **4 chicken bouillon cubes dissolved in 1 cup boiling water**
>
> **½ cup firmly packed creamy-style peanut butter**
>
> **¼ cup soy sauce**
>
> **3 tablespoons distilled white vinegar**
>
> **2 tablespoons firmly packed dark brown sugar**
>
> **1 medium red bell pepper, diced**
>
> **⅓ cup finely chopped fresh cilantro**
>
> **3 scallions, thinly sliced on the diagonal**

Bring 2 quarts of water to a boil in a 6- to 8-quart pot over high heat. Stir in the pasta and return to a boil. Boil, stirring occasionally, until the pasta is al dente (slightly firm to the bite), 6 to 9 minutes. Drain the pasta in a colander. Transfer to a shallow serving bowl and toss with the oil until the pasta is well coated. Set aside.

Add the peanuts to a medium (10- to 12-inch) cast-iron skillet and place over medium heat. Dry-toast the peanuts, tossing, until light golden brown, 3 minutes.

Pour in the hot chicken bouillon and stir in the peanut butter, soy sauce, vinegar, brown sugar, and red bell pepper until well blended. Cook, stirring, until the mixture is well blended and the brown sugar and peanut butter are dissolved, 1 minute. (You may see "flecks" of peanut butter, but they will dissolve completely once the sauce is stirred into the pasta.)

Add the sauce to the bowl with the pasta and gently toss along with the cilantro and scallions until well blended. Serve at room temperature.

ZUCCHINI ROMANO

YOU CAN ALSO MAKE THIS simple yet gratifying dish with fresh yellow summer squash.

2 tablespoons olive oil

1 pound medium zucchini, thinly sliced

3 cloves garlic, crushed through a garlic press

⅓ cup freshly grated Romano cheese

Salt and freshly ground pepper, to taste

Heat the oil in a large (12- to 14-inch) cast-iron skillet over medium high heat for 1 minute. Add the zucchini and sauté until tender and golden brown, 4 to 6 minutes.

Transfer the zucchini to a warmed serving bowl and toss with the garlic and Romano cheese until well blended. Season with salt and pepper and serve at once.

SCALLOPED POTATOES

YOU CAN'T GO WRONG WITH potatoes, and this side dish is very flexible in that it is the perfect punctuation to almost any entrée.

1 tablespoon unsalted butter, to grease

2 pounds baking potatoes

3 tablespoons all-purpose flour

½ teaspoon salt

½ teaspoon freshly ground black pepper

1½ cups milk, heated

1 cup diced onion

3 tablespoons minced fresh chives

5 strips bacon, cooked and crumbled

3 tablespoons unsalted butter, melted

Salt and freshly ground pepper, to taste

Preheat the oven to 375F (190C). Generously grease the bottom and sides of a medium (10- to 12-inch) cast-iron skillet with the butter.

Peel the potatoes and slice them very thinly. As you slice them, quickly submerge them in a large bowl of ice water.

In a small bowl, mix the flour, salt, and pepper until well blended. Whisk in the heated milk until well blended.

Drain the potatoes and place half of them in the prepared skillet by slightly overlapping them in a pattern of concentric circles. Top with an even layer of the onion, sprinkle with the chives and bacon, drizzle with half of the melted butter, and pour the milk mixture over all. Top with the remaining potatoes arranged in concentric circles and drizzle with the remaining butter.

Cover with a lid and bake for 45 minutes. Uncover and bake for 30 to 35 minutes more or until the potatoes are tender when pierced with a fork, the top is dappled golden brown, and the edges are crispy. Season with salt and pepper and serve hot directly from the skillet.

SUCCOTASH

IF YOU'VE NEVER HAD THE Southern favorite succotash, you are in for a real treat!

2 cups fresh lima beans or 1 (9-ounce) package frozen lima beans

1 ounce salt pork (page 112)

1 to 1¼ cups water, or as needed

½ teaspoon sugar

1 teaspoon salt

½ teaspoon freshly ground pepper

2 cups fresh corn kernels or 1 (9-ounce) package frozen corn kernels

1 tablespoon all-purpose flour

⅓ cup heavy cream, at room temperature

In a large (12- to 14-inch) cast-iron skillet over medium heat, combine the lima beans, salt pork, 1 cup water, sugar, salt, and pepper. Stir until combined, cover, and bring to a boil.

Reduce heat to medium-low, cover, and simmer until the lima beans are just tender, 10 to 15 minutes. Stir in the corn. Add up to ¼ cup more water if needed to just cover. Cover and simmer until the corn is tender, about 5 minutes. Remove and discard the salt pork.

Meanwhile, in a small bowl, whisk together the flour and cream until well blended and smooth. Gradually stir into the skillet until well blended and cook, stirring constantly, until the mixture has thickened, 3 to 4 minutes. Serve at once.

SWEET POTATO-CARROT PUDDING

Makes 6 servings

THE CONSISTENCY OF THIS OLD-TIME recipe is between a spoon bread and a bread pudding; you serve it with a spoon, but you're tempted to use a knife.

1 tablespoon unsalted butter, to grease

3 cups firmly packed, mashed cooked carrots (made from 1½ pounds peeled, trimmed raw carrots)

3 cups firmly packed, mashed cooked sweet potatoes (made from 2 pounds peeled raw sweet potatoes)

3 cups unseasoned dry bread crumbs

6 tablespoons firmly packed light brown sugar

1 teaspoon ground cinnamon

1 teaspoon salt

3 large eggs, beaten

4 cups milk

Preheat the oven to 350F (175C). Grease the interior of a large (12- to 14-inch) cast-iron skillet with the butter.

Combine the carrots, sweet potatoes, bread crumbs, sugar, cinnamon, and salt in a large bowl and stir until well blended. Stir in the eggs and milk until well blended.

Pour into the prepared skillet. Bake on the center oven rack for 45 to 50 minutes, or until puffed and a knife comes out almost clean (with a few moist crumbs, but not wet batter clinging to it) when inserted in the center. Serve at once directly from the skillet.

SWISS CHARD WITH FRESH FENNEL

THE COMBINATION OF SWISS CHARD and fresh fennel is surprisingly right. The impact of the tender chard, sweet, plump raisins, and nutty balsamic vinegar is the perfect foil to the slight crunch of the delicately anise-flavored fennel. Balsamic vinegar is available from Italian grocery stores and most supermarkets.

> **2 tablespoons olive oil**
>
> **1 medium yellow onion, minced**
>
> **2 cloves garlic, crushed through a garlic press**
>
> **1 medium bulb fresh fennel (about 1¼ pounds), trimmed and thinly sliced, reserving feathery leaves for the garnish**
>
> **½ cup water**
>
> **1 bunch Swiss chard (about 8 ounces), leaves torn into bite-sized pieces**
>
> **⅔ cup raisins**
>
> **2 tablespoons balsamic vinegar**
>
> **Salt and freshly ground pepper, to taste**

Heat the oil in a medium (10- to 12-inch) cast-iron skillet over medium heat for 1 minute. Add the onion and garlic and cook, stirring often, until the onion is tender, 4 minutes.

Add the fennel and water and cook, stirring often, until crisp-tender, about 6 minutes. Stir in the Swiss chard and cook, stirring often, until the Swiss chard leaves have wilted, about 5 minutes. (If the Swiss chard leaves clump together, separate with a fork.)

Transfer the mixture to a serving bowl. Add the raisins and balsamic vinegar and stir until well blended. Season with salt and pepper and garnish with the reserved fennel fronds. Serve at once.

DEEP-FRIED TOFU TRIANGLES
WITH GINGER-MISO SAUCE

Makes 4 servings

GOLDEN TRIANGLES OF FRIED TOFU crowned with this thick spicy sauce are altogether sensational.

SAUCE

¼ cup red miso (available at Japanese grocery stores or health food stores)

3 tablespoons mirin (Japanese rice wine), available at Japanese grocery stores or health food stores

3 tablespoons light brown sugar

1 tablespoon freshly grated peeled ginger

2 cloves garlic, crushed through a garlic press

1 tablespoon sesame oil

¼ teaspoon dry mustard

TOFU

15 ounces (drained weight) firm-style tofu, each cake cut crosswise into ½-inch-thick slices, then cut in half on the diagonal to form 2 triangles per slice (available at health food stores or supermarkets)

⅓ cup cornstarch, to dust

4 to 6 cups peanut oil, to fry

Salt and freshly ground pepper, to season

2 scallions, sliced thinly on the diagonal, to garnish

TO MAKE THE SAUCE: Combine the sauce ingredients in a medium bowl and stir until well blended. Set aside at room temperature until ready to serve.

TO PREPARE THE TOFU: Lay the tofu out on paper towels and gently pat the tofu very dry. Transfer the cornstarch to a sieve and dust both sides of the tofu until evenly coated.

Preheat the oven to 200F (95C). Pour the oil in a cast-iron wok to a depth of 3 inches. Heat the oil over medium-high heat until a deep-fry thermometer registers 365F (185C). Add the tofu in batches (do not crowd the wok) and fry until the exterior is crisp and golden brown, 1 to 2 minutes on each side.

Using tongs, transfer the tofu to a paper towel-lined plate to drain, then to a baking sheet lined with foil and hold them in the warm oven until all batches are ready. Use a slotted spoon to skim the surface of the oil in between batches to keep it clean.

Sprinkle with salt and pepper, drizzle with the sauce, and garnish with the scallions. Serve at once.

TABBOULEH TOMATOES

Makes 6 servings

CAST IRON HEATS THE TOMATOES evenly without allowing them to burst.

1 (6-ounce) package tabbouleh mix (available from health food stores or supermarkets)

1 cup cold water

2 tablespoons olive oil

2 tablespoons fresh lemon juice

½ cup minced fresh basil or marjoram

Salt and freshly ground pepper, to taste

6 large tomatoes (Choose tomatoes with flat bottoms so they can easily stand up in the skillet.)

¼ cup freshly grated Parmesan cheese

Stir together the tabbouleh mix, water, oil, lemon juice, and basil in a medium bowl until well blended. Season with salt and pepper.

Slice the top ¼ inch off each tomato, discard the stem piece and dice the caps. Stir the diced tomato into the tabbouleh mixture until well blended. Cover the bowl and let stand for 30 minutes.

Meanwhile, using a spoon, seed the tomatoes (reserving the pulp and juice for another use), leaving ¼ inch-thick shells and reserve until ready to use.

Preheat the oven to 350F (175C). Using a spoon, firmly pack each tomato shell full with the tabbouleh mixture. Sprinkle each evenly with the Parmesan cheese and arrange the tomatoes upright in a medium (10- to 12-inch) cast iron skillet. Bake for 10 to 15 minutes or just until heated through, and serve.

Peerless Fried Green Tomatoes

Makes 4 servings

I SERVE FRIED GREEN TOMATOES with a small dollop of Sauce Rémoulade on the center of each. If you dare, slip a strip of bacon into the oil as you add the tomatoes for even richer flavor; it's best that way!

1 large egg, beaten

2 tablespoons milk

½ teaspoon salt

¼ teaspoon freshly ground pepper

½ cup all-purpose flour

¾ cup yellow cornmeal

3 to 5 cups vegetable oil, to fry

4 firm medium green (unripe) tomatoes, cored and cut into 12 slices

Salt and freshly ground pepper, to season

Sauce Rémoulade (see below), to serve

In a medium bowl, combine the egg, milk, salt, and pepper and whisk until well blended. In another medium bowl, stir together the flour and cornmeal until well blended.

Preheat the oven to 200F (95C). Pour the oil into a large (12- to 14-inch) cast-iron skillet to reach a ¾-inch depth and set over medium-high heat. Heat the oil until a deep-fry thermometer registers 350F (175C).

One by one, dip the tomato slices in the egg mixture to coat evenly. Then dip in the cornmeal mixture, shaking off any excess and placing on a sheet of waxed paper.

Fry the tomatoes in batches (do not crowd the skillet) until the coating is crisp and light golden brown, 1 to 3 minutes on each side.

Working quickly, using tongs, transfer the tomatoes to a paper towel-lined baking sheet to drain. Then transfer to a baking sheet lined with foil and hold them in the warm oven until all the batches are ready. Use a slotted spoon to skim the surface of the oil between batches to keep it clean. Season the tomatoes with salt and pepper and serve with a small dollop of Sauce Rémoulade on the center of each slice.

SAUCE RÉMOULADE

1 cup mayonnaise, preferably homemade

2 tablespoons finely chopped fresh tarragon

2 tablespoons finely chopped fresh chervil or fresh chives

2 tablespoons finely chopped fresh parsley

1 tablespoon Dijon mustard

2 heaping tablespoons minced sweet gherkin pickles

1 tablespoon plus 1 teaspoon finely chopped capers

½ teaspoon anchovy paste or 2 anchovy fillets, minced and using a fork, mashed to form a paste

Combine all the ingredients in a small bowl and stir until well blended. Cover and refrigerate until ready to use.

WESTPHALIAN GREEN BEANS WITH SWEET-SOUR WARM DRESSING

Makes 4 servings

THE SMOKY FLAVOR OF BACON makes a superlative backdrop to this sweet-sour dish that I adore, and I hope you will, too.

8 strips bacon

1 medium yellow onion, finely chopped

1 (9-ounce) package frozen French-cut green beans, thawed

⅛ cup water

2 tablespoons apple cider vinegar

1 tablespoon sugar

½ teaspoon salt

Add the bacon to a medium (10- to 12-inch) cast-iron skillet over medium heat. Fry the bacon until crisp, 4 to 6 minutes. Using tongs, remove the bacon, leaving the drippings in the skillet, and transfer to paper towels. Crumble and reserve the bacon until ready to use.

Place the skillet with the drippings over medium heat and add the onion, green beans, and water. Cook, stirring occasionally, until the green beans and onion are tender but not browned, 4 to 6 minutes.

Stir in the vinegar, sugar, and salt. Sprinkle with the reserved bacon and serve at once.

BAKED WHOLE ONIONS
FINISHED WITH MARSALA

CAST IRON IS THE PERFECT medium for roasting foods, as it holds heat so well and distributes the heat evenly.

- **6 medium-sized yellow or other onions, about 3 inches in diameter**
- **4 tablespoons (½ stick) unsalted butter, melted**
- **½ cup dry Marsala (an Italian fortified wine)**
- **1 teaspoon salt**
- **½ teaspoon freshly ground pepper**

Preheat the oven to 400F (205C). Cut a very thin slice from the root end of each onion so that it can stand upright, but don't penetrate into the interior of the bulb. Cut a very thin slice off the top to remove the stem. Peel, and cut an X 2 inches deep into each onion top.

Arrange the onions, root ends down, in a single layer in a medium (10- to 12-inch) cast-iron skillet.

Stir together the butter, Marsala, salt, and pepper in a small bowl until well blended to make a glaze.

Spoon the glaze evenly over the onions and loosely tent the baking dish with foil. (Cover with the foil, but do not let the foil rest on the onions.)

Bake the onions in the center of the oven for about 1½ hours, basting with the glaze every 30 minutes, or until the onions are very tender when pierced with a fork in the thickest part. Transfer to a serving dish, spoon the glaze over the onions, and serve.

ZUCCHINI QUINOA

Makes 4 to 6 servings

ONE OF THE INGREDIENTS THAT I know you'll be seeing more of is quinoa, the grain supercharged-with-nutrition. I chose to partner zucchini and quinoa in this dish because the squash flavor of zucchini echoes the faint squashlike flavor of quinoa. It is mandatory to rinse and drain the quinoa prior to using, or it will have an unpleasantly bitter taste. Quinoa is available at health-food stores.

⅓ **cup olive oil**

1 medium yellow onion, minced

3 cloves garlic, crushed through a garlic press

1 cup thinly sliced celery

1 medium red bell pepper, diced

1½ pounds small zucchini, thinly sliced

2¼ cups canned vegetable broth

1 cup quinoa, rinsed and drained

¾ **cup freshly grated Romano cheese**

Salt and freshly ground pepper, to taste

Heat the oil in a large (12- to 14-inch) cast-iron skillet over medium heat for 1 minute. Add the onion, garlic, celery, bell pepper, and zucchini and cook, stirring often, until the zucchini is tender when pierced with a fork, 10 to 15 minutes. Remove the skillet from the heat, cover, and reserve until ready to use.

Stir together the vegetable broth and quinoa in a 2- to 3-quart saucepan. Place the saucepan over medium-high heat and bring the mixture to a boil.

Reduce the heat to medium-low, cover, and simmer, stirring often, until the quinoa is translucent and the outer germ rings separate, 20 to 30 minutes.

Stir the quinoa along with the Romano cheese into the reserved zucchini mixture and season with salt and pepper. Return the skillet with the zucchini quinoa mixture to low heat. Cook, stirring, until heated through, about 3 minutes, and serve.

BUTTERNUT SQUASH RISOTTO WITH DRIED CRANBERRIES AND SAGE, TOPPED WITH TOASTED PINE NUTS

Makes 4 servings

EVER SINCE I DEVELOPED THIS recipe from some notes I penned in my kitchen diary last Thanksgiving, it has become a telegram to me of the autumnal cornucopia of ingredients available to us. The wealth of color displayed in this dish, from the orange butternut squash to the sparkle of the dried ruby red cranberries, is now a permanent fixture of my Thanksgiving feast.

1¾ ounces (⅓ cup plus 1 tablespoon) pine nuts, also called *pignoli*

3 tablespoons unsalted butter

1 medium yellow onion, finely chopped

1 (1-pound) butternut squash, peeled, trimmed, cut in half lengthwise, stringy pulp and seeds discarded, and cut into ½-inch cubes

1 tablespoon olive oil

1 cup Arborio rice (available at gourmet shops or Italian grocery stores)

4 vegetable bouillon cubes dissolved in 2 cups boiling water

¾ cup dry white wine

⅔ cup dried cranberries (available at gourmet shops and most supermarkets)

½ cup freshly grated Parmesan cheese

¾ teaspoon dried sage

Salt and freshly ground pepper, to taste

Place a medium (4- to 6-quart) cast-iron Dutch oven over medium heat. Add the pine nuts and dry-toast, stirring constantly, until light golden brown, 3 to 5 minutes. Remove and reserve.

Return the Dutch oven to medium heat and melt the butter. Add the onion and butternut squash and cook, stirring often, until the squash is fork tender, 10 to 15 minutes. Reserve until ready to use.

Add the oil to the Dutch oven and heat for 1 minute. Stir in the rice and cook, stirring frequently, until well coated, 2 minutes.

Stir in ½ cup of the vegetable bouillon and the wine (caution: mixture will splatter). Cook, stirring often, until the liquid has been completely absorbed, 3 to 5 minutes.

Add another ½ cup vegetable bouillon and cook, stirring frequently, until all but a few tablespoons of the liquid has been absorbed, 3 to 5 minutes. Continue adding the bouillon in ½ cup amounts and cooking, stirring frequently, until the liquid is nearly absorbed. This will take 15 to 20 minutes cooking time. The rice should be creamy and al dente (slightly firm to the bite). (Each addition of bouillon will take slightly longer to be absorbed. The longer the rice cooks, the longer it takes to absorb liquid.) Do not leave the dish unattended.

Working quickly, remove the Dutch oven from the heat and stir in the reserved squash mixture along with the dried cranberries and Parmesan cheese. Rub the sage between your fingers (to release its aroma), add to the Dutch oven, and stir until well blended. Season with salt and pepper.

Transfer to a warm serving bowl, sprinkle with the reserved pine nuts, and serve at once.

Sweet Potato Fries with Homemade Ketchup

Makes 6 servings

THIS RECIPE IS INSPIRED FROM Chris Schlesinger's and John Willoughby's *License to Grill* cookbook. Although their idea of sweet potato fries with homemade ketchup is not a new one altogether, I thought their technique of baking the spuds first before frying was a more foolproof method to preparing classic steak fries using sweet potatoes instead of white potatoes.

4 medium sweet potatoes (about 3 pounds), peeled, cut lengthwise into eighths, then cut crosswise to make 16 wedges per potato

7 to 9 cups corn oil, for frying

Salt and freshly ground pepper, to taste

Homemade Ketchup (see below)

Preheat the oven to 400F (205C). Arrange the sweet potato wedges in a single layer on a baking sheet. Bake for 25 to 30 minutes, or until tender when pierced with a fork in the thickest part, yet still firm (not hard) in the center.

Reduce oven temperature to 200F (95C). Pour the oil into a medium (4- to 6-quart) cast-iron Dutch oven to a depth of 3 inches. Heat the oil over medium-high heat until a deep-fry thermometer registers 350F (175C).

Fry the sweet potato wedges in batches (do not crowd the Dutch oven), turning them in the oil often, until they turn light golden brown and the exterior is crisp, 2 to 4 minutes.

Using a slotted spoon, transfer the fries to a paper towel-lined plate to drain, then to a baking sheet lined with foil, and hold them in the warm oven until all the batches are ready. Serve at once seasoned with salt and pepper with the Homemade Ketchup on the side.

HOMEMADE KETCHUP

1¼ pounds tomatoes, finely chopped

1 cup canned tomato puree

1 cup distilled white vinegar

½ cup molasses

¼ cup firmly packed dark brown sugar

1 (½-inch-long) stick cinnamon

1 medium yellow onion, finely chopped

6 cloves garlic, crushed through a garlic press

2 teaspoons ground allspice

½ to 1 teaspoon Worcestershire sauce, or to taste

¼ teaspoon ground cloves

¼ teaspoon ground mace

Salt and freshly ground pepper, to taste

Combine all the ingredients in a 3- to 4-quart stainless-steel pot and stir until well combined. Place over medium-high heat and bring to a boil, stirring occasionally.

Reduce the heat to low and simmer for 1 hour, stirring often. Remove and discard the cinnamon stick. Remove from the heat and let cool completely.

Puree in a food processor fitted with the stainless-steel blade or in a blender until smooth. Transfer to a large glass or stainless-steel bowl, cover, and refrigerate until ready to serve. Store in an airtight container in the refrigerator for up to 1 week.

CHILI POWDER-DUSTED
FRIED ONION RINGS

Makes 6 servings

YOU CAN USE THE ONION of your choice for this recipe. These onion rings have a fantastic full beer flavor with just a hint of chili taste (but not enough to add heat) in the background for flavor depth.

> 2 cups chilled buttermilk
>
> 1 cup beer
>
> 3 cups all-purpose flour
>
> 2 teaspoons chili powder
>
> 3 medium onions (about 1½ pounds total), cut into ¼ inch-thick slices and each slice separated into rings
>
> 7 to 9 cups peanut oil, to fry
>
> Salt and freshly ground pepper, to taste

Whisk together the buttermilk, beer, flour, and chili powder in a large bowl until well blended. Dip the onion rings into the mixture until evenly coated with the batter, very gently shaking off any excess, then lay in a single layer onto a large sheet of waxed paper.

Preheat the oven to 200F (95C). Pour the oil into a medium (4- to 6 quart) cast-iron Dutch oven to a depth of 3 inches. Heat the oil over medium high heat until a deep-fry thermometer registers 375F (190C).

Fry the onion rings in batches (do not crowd the Dutch oven), turning them in the oil often, until they turn golden brown and the batter puffs up and forms a crispy crust, about 1 minute on each side. Use a slotted spoon to skim the surface of the oil in between batches to keep it clean.

Using tongs, transfer the onion rings to a paper towel-lined plate to drain, then to a baking sheet lined with foil, and hold them in the warm oven until all the batches are ready. Season with salt and pepper and serve at once.

FRIED BABY OKRA

THOUGH OKRA IS A FAVORED ingredient in many famous dishes of the South, it does have a texture that some folks just don't fall in love with. However, even if you aren't smitten with okra, do try this old-time preparation and give okra another whirl.

2 large eggs

½ cup beer

1 tablespoon corn oil

¾ cup all-purpose flour

1 teaspoon salt

1 teaspoon freshly ground black pepper

½ teaspoon cayenne pepper

1 pound fresh whole baby okra

1 tablespoon baking powder

7 to 9 cups peanut oil, to fry

In a large bowl, whisk together the eggs, beer, corn oil, flour, salt, black pepper, and cayenne until well blended. Cover and refrigerate for 2 hours before using.

Just before frying, trim off and discard the ends of the okra. Cut the okra into ¼-inch-thick slices.

Whisk the baking powder into the batter until well blended, then stir in the okra until well coated.

Preheat the oven to 200F (95C). Pour the peanut oil into a medium (4- to 6-quart) cast-iron Dutch oven to a depth of 3 inches. Heat the oil over medium-high heat until a deep-fry thermometer reads 375F (190C).

Drop each batter-covered okra individually into the oil. Fry the okra in batches (do not crowd the Dutch oven), turning them in the oil often, until they turn light golden brown and the batter forms a crisp crust, 30 seconds to 1 minute on each side.

Using a slotted spoon, transfer the okra to a paper towel-lined plate to drain, then to a baking sheet lined with foil, and hold them in the warm oven until all the batches are ready. Serve at once.

SIDE DISHES

Caramelized Onion and Fig Tart

Makes 4 to 6 servings

THIS OPEN-FACED TART IS intensely flavored with a very rich crust and is perfect as an appetizer or hors d'oeuvre. For a light luncheon: Plate a slice of this tart with a wedge of Gorgonzola cheese and ripe pear, which counterpoises the sweet-like-candy caramelized onion topping. The topping can be made up to 3 days ahead. Let it cool, put it in an airtight container, and refrigerate.

CRUST

    1½ cups all-purpose flour

    1 teaspoon salt

    1 stick (½ cup) unsalted butter, cut into ½-inch cubes, chilled

    1 large egg yolk whisked with 2 tablespoons cold water

    3 to 4 tablespoons ice water

FILLING

    2 teaspoons extra-virgin olive oil

    ½ pound yellow onions, thinly sliced

    1 cup water

    1 tablespoon sugar

    Salt and freshly ground pepper, to taste

    1¼ cups finely chopped dried figs (stems removed)

TO MAKE THE DOUGH: Sift together the flour and salt in a medium bowl. Using a pastry blender or fork, cut in the chilled butter until mixture resembles coarse crumbs. Stir in the egg yolk-water mixture until well blended. Sprinkle in the 3 tablespoons water, a little at a time, adding more if necessary, just enough for the mixture to gather together to form a dough but not become sticky.

Form into a flat disk, wrap in waxed paper and then plastic wrap, and refrigerate for at least 30 minutes, preferably overnight.

MEANWHILE, TO MAKE THE TOPPING: Heat the oil in a 12- to 14-inch cast-iron skillet over medium heat for 1 minute. Add the onions and sauté for 2 minutes.

Add the water and cook, stirring often, until the water is evaporated, 15 minutes.

Reduce the heat to low, stir in the sugar, and cook, stirring often, until the onion is a deep golden brown and begins to fall apart and form a thick puree, 10 to 12 minutes. Season with salt and pepper. Cover and reserve until ready to use.

Preheat the oven to 425F (220C). On a lightly floured work surface, roll out the dough into a 12-inch-diameter circle, trimming any rough edges. Transfer the dough to an ungreased 10-inch cast-iron skillet and line the skillet with the dough, allowing the dough to come up the side.

Using your fingers, gently spread the onions in an even layer over the dough. (The onion layer will be thin.) Using a fork, prick the surface of the tart (through the filling) all over to keep the crust flat while baking, and scatter the figs over the onions. Season the topping with salt and pepper. Fold about ½ inch of the dough's edge over onto the topping, leaving an opening of exposed topping in the center of the tart.

Bake on the center rack of the oven for 15 to 20 minutes or until the edge of the crust is crisp and a delicate brown. (Watch the tart carefully; if it starts to bubble and the crust begins to lift off the skillet, use a fork to prick the surface again all over.)

Remove from the oven and let stand for 10 minutes. Run a small, sharp knife along the crust edge to help loosen it from the skillet. Using a pizza wheel or serrated knife, cut into wedges and, using a spatula, carefully remove (so as not to break) and serve hot or at room temperature.

BREADS

JONNYCAKES TOPPED WITH BÉARNAISE SAUCE

Makes 8 to 12 (3-inch) jonnycakes

YOU CAN EAT JONNYCAKES OUT of your hand. I love them so much I'll eat them cold after I've already had a full plate of them hot with melted butter and fruit syrup or preserves for breakfast. Though not traditional, I have suggested topping them with Béarnaise Sauce for an appetizer, which puts them in another class altogether.

1 cup white cornmeal

½ teaspoon salt

¼ cup boiling water

½ cup milk

5 tablespoons heavy cream

Corn oil, to fry

Béarnaise Sauce (see below), to serve

Fresh tarragon leaves, to garnish

In a medium bowl, stir together the cornmeal and salt until blended. Using a fork, stir in the boiling water until well blended. Stir in the milk and cream until the batter is smooth.

Preheat oven to 200F (95C). Brush a cast-iron griddle with a generous amount of oil and heat over medium-high heat until hot enough to make drops of water dance over the surface, 2 minutes.

Working in batches, pour about ¼ cup of batter for each jonnycake onto the griddle, forming 3-inch rounds. Cook the jonnycakes until the undersides are golden and the tops are bubbly, 3 to 5 minutes. Flip the jonnycakes over and cook until lightly brown and the outsides are crispy, 1 to 3 minutes.

Repeat with remaining batter, brushing the griddle generously with the oil in between batches and holding the jonnycakes on a baking sheet in the warm oven while cooking the remaining batter. Top the center of each jonnycake with a small dollop of the Béarnaise Sauce and a tarragon leaf, and serve at once.

BÉARNAISE SAUCE

Makes about 1¼ cups

IF THE EGGS SCRAMBLE WHILE you make this classic French sauce, there are tricks to "save" the sauce, but, quite frankly, I believe it's best just to start over. And there isn't that much of a risk of scrambling if you whisk constantly and keep the water barely simmering.

¾ **cup dry white wine**

¼ **cup white wine vinegar**

4 **ounces shallots, finely chopped**

1 **tablespoon minced fresh tarragon**

¼ **teaspoon salt**

¾ **teaspoon freshly ground pepper**

4 **large egg yolks, at room temperature**

2 **sticks (1 cup) unsalted butter, cut into ½-inch cubes**

In a 2- to 3-quart stainless-steel saucepan, stir together the wine, vinegar, shallots, tarragon, salt, and pepper until combined. Place over high heat and boil until the mixture has reduced to about 3 tablespoons of liquid, 7 to 9 minutes.

Strain the liquid through a fine-meshed sieve into the upper pan of a stainless-steel double boiler and set aside to cool completely.

Whisk the egg yolks into the liquid until well blended and place over the bottom pan of the double boiler partially filled with barely simmering water over low heat.

While whisking constantly, add the butter a piece at a time, making sure each piece has melted before adding another piece, and scraping the sides of the pan as you whisk. (Whisk constantly so that the eggs don't scramble.) Continue whisking until all the butter is incorporated and the sauce is smooth with a glossy sheen.

Remove the top pan from the bottom pan, whisking often to prevent the sauce from breaking or forming a skin, and serve at once.

SOPAIPILLAS WITH HONEY BUTTER

Makes 6 to 8 servings

I HAVE TASTE-TESTED MANY TYPES of this Southwestern specialty, and I like this version best—crisp, puffy, air-filled "pillows" of deep-fried pastry. They must be enjoyed warm, though once your guests get a whiff of their fragrance, I doubt the sopaipillas will have a fleeting chance of getting cold.

3 cups all-purpose flour

1 teaspoon baking powder

1 (¼-ounce) package active dry yeast

¼ cup warm water (110 to 115F; 40 to 45C)

1 cup milk

2 tablespoons lard or solid vegetable shortening

1 teaspoon salt

2 teaspoons sugar

1 stick (½ cup) plus 1 teaspoon unsalted butter

6 tablespoons honey

½ teaspoon ground cinnamon

7 to 9 cups peanut oil, to fry

Sift the flour and baking powder into a large bowl and reserve until ready to use.

Sprinkle the yeast over the warm water, stir until the yeast is dissolved, and set aside for 5 minutes.

Meanwhile, combine the milk, lard, salt, and sugar in a 2- to 3-quart saucepan. Place over medium heat and heat, whisking often, until sugar and lard are dissolved, the mixture is well blended, and an instant-read thermometer registers 110 to 115F (40 to 45C). Stir in the yeast mixture until well blended.

Pour the wet ingredients into the reserved flour mixture and mix until the mixture gathers into a soft dough. Transfer to a lightly floured work surface and knead until smooth and elastic, 8 to 10 minutes.

Grease a large, deep bowl with the 1 teaspoon butter. Add the dough and turn it to coat with the butter. Cover the dough with a kitchen towel and let stand for 20 minutes.

Meanwhile, combine the ½ cup butter, honey, and cinnamon in a 1- to 2-quart saucepan set over low heat. Heat, stirring, until the butter is melted and the mixture is well blended, 1 to 2 minutes. Remove from the heat and reserve, covered, to keep warm until ready to serve.

On a lightly floured work surface, roll out the dough to a ¼-inch thickness and cut into 3-inch squares. Then cut each square on the diagonal to make 2 triangles per square. Re-roll the scraps and repeat the process until you have a total of about 50 triangles.

Preheat the oven to 200F (95C). Pour the oil into a medium (4- to 6-quart) cast-iron Dutch oven to a depth of 3 inches and set over medium-high heat. Heat the oil until it reads 375F (190C) on a deep-fry thermometer.

Fry the sopaipillas in batches (do not crowd the Dutch oven), 7 to 8 at a time, turning them in the oil often, until lightly golden brown and puffed all over, about 30 seconds to 1 minute on each side.

Working quickly, using a slotted spoon, transfer the sopaipillas to a paper towel-lined baking sheet to drain. Then transfer to a baking sheet lined with foil and hold in the warm oven until all the batches are ready.

Serve the sopaipillas at once, passing with the reserved honey butter for dipping.

ETHEREAL SPOON BREAD

SPOON BREAD IS LIKE A soufflé in that it is light and airy, but a spoon bread is not as fragile. It is best eaten as soon as it's baked, good and warm. Sprinkle it with salt and pepper just before serving, whether for a dinner or luncheon side dish. I have served it dusted with confectioners' sugar and alongside fresh fruit salad for an unusual but now popular brunch dish among my frequent guests.

> **4 large egg yolks**
> **3 cups canned evaporated milk**
> **½ cup cold water**
> **1 cup yellow cornmeal**
> **3 tablespoons unsalted butter**
> **5 large egg whites**

Preheat the oven to 375F (190C). Generously coat the bottom (not the sides) of a medium (4- to 6-quart) cast-iron Dutch oven with nonstick cooking spray.

In a large heatproof bowl, whisk the egg yolks until beaten and reserve.

Combine ½ cup of the evaporated milk and the cold water in a large measuring cup. Add the cornmeal and whisk until well blended. In a 3- to 4-quart saucepan over medium-low heat, bring the remaining 2½ cups evaporated milk to a boil, whisking occasionally. Reduce the heat to low, and gradually pour in the cornmeal mixture in a slow, steady stream while whisking vigorously and constantly to blend well.

Cook, whisking, just until mixture becomes smooth, thick, and stiff and begins to pull away from the sides of the pan, 1 to 4 minutes. The mixture will be very thick and fairly difficult to whisk.

Working quickly, remove the saucepan from the heat and whisk in the butter until the butter has melted and is blended.

Whisk one-fourth of the hot cornmeal mixture into the bowl of egg yolks until well blended and smooth. Then whisk in the remaining cornmeal mixture until blended and smooth.

Place the prepared Dutch oven in the center of the oven and heat.

In a large bowl, beat the egg whites with an electric mixer on high speed until stiff, glossy (not dry) peaks form, and the peaks hold their shape when the beaters are raised upside down, about 3 minutes.

Working quickly, whisk one-fourth of the beaten egg whites into the cornmeal mixture until well blended. Using a rubber spatula, gently fold the remaining egg whites into the cornmeal mixture just until blended.

Pour the mixture into the hot Dutch oven, smooth the surface, and bake for 25 to 30 minutes or until puffy and light golden brown on the top. The interior will be soft and fluffy, while the surface and edges will be crispy. Serve at once directly from the Dutch oven.

PECAN-CINNAMON STICKY BUNS

YOU'LL WANT TO WAKE UP to these pull-apart buns. A good shot of bourbon blends with the other ingredients for a richer dimension. But don't expect a strong flavor like a rum-spiked cake—the bourbon adds more of a mellow, background note to the cinnamon and pecans and the welcoming flavor of yeast.

  3½ to 4 cups all-purpose flour
  1 (¼-ounce) package active dry yeast
  1 cup milk
  1 cup sugar
  ¼ cup solid vegetable shortening
  1 teaspoon salt
  1 tablespoon plus 1 teaspoon ground cinnamon
  1¾ cups coarsely chopped pecans
  2 large eggs, beaten
  4 tablespoons (½ stick) plus 1 teaspoon unsalted butter
  ⅔ cup firmly packed dark brown sugar
  2 tablespoons light corn syrup
  ¼ cup bourbon

In a large mixing bowl, stir together 2 cups of the flour and the yeast with an electric mixer until well blended.

In a 2- to 3-quart saucepan, combine the milk, ¼ cup of the granulated sugar, shortening, and salt and place over low heat. Heat, whisking often, until the sugar and shortening are dissolved and an instant-read thermometer registers 110 to 115F (40 to 45C).

Meanwhile, stir together the cinnamon, ¾ cup of the pecans, and the remaining ¾ cup granulated sugar in a small bowl until well combined and reserve until ready to use.

Using an electric mixer fitted with a paddle, beat the milk mixture into the flour-yeast mixture in the bowl until just blended. Add the eggs and beat on low speed for 30 seconds. Scrape down the sides of the bowl using a rubber spatula, then beat for 3 minutes on high speed.

Using a wooden spoon, stir in enough of the remaining 1½ to 2 cups flour to make a moderately stiff dough. Knead the dough on a lightly floured work surface until the dough is smooth and elastic, 8 to 10 minutes. Shape into a ball.

Grease a large, deep bowl with the 1 teaspoon of butter and add the dough. Turn the dough to coat it with the butter. Let the dough rise, covered with a kitchen towel, in a warm place for 1 hour or until doubled in bulk.

Punch down dough and divide in half. Cover the dough halves and let rest for 10 minutes.

On a lightly floured work surface, roll each half to a 12 × 8 inch rectangle. Sprinkle half of the reserved cinnamon mixture evenly over the top of each of the 2 rectangles.

Roll each up, jelly-roll style, starting with a long side. Pinch the edges together to seal the seam. Using a serrated knife, slice each roll into 12 pieces.

Combine the brown sugar, 4 tablespoons butter, corn syrup, and bourbon in a 1- to 2-quart saucepan over low heat. Cook, stirring, until the butter melts and the brown sugar dissolves, 3 minutes.

Pour the mixture into a large (12- to 14-inch) cast-iron skillet and sprinkle with the remaining 1 cup of pecans.

Transfer the buns to the skillet, which should be large enough to accommodate the buns in a single layer; they should touch one another snugly. Sprinkle with any cinnamon mixture that may have fallen out while transferring the buns. Cover with a kitchen towel and let rise in a warm place about 30 minutes or until double in size.

Meanwhile, preheat the oven to 375F (190C). Bake the buns in the center of the oven for 18 to 20 minutes or until delicately browned on top. (Watch carefully so as not to overcook or the bottom will burn.)

Let cool in the skillet on a wire rack for 30 seconds. Run a small, sharp knife around the edge of the buns to loosen from the skillet. Invert the buns as a group (do not separate) onto a serving platter. Scrape out and drizzle any topping and pecans remaining in the skillet on the buns and serve at once.

OLD-TIME HUSHPUPPIES WITH VIETNAMESE-STYLE DIPPING SAUCE

Makes 6 servings

THOUGH IT ISN'T TRADITIONAL BY any means, I like to serve hushpuppies with a dipping sauce. If you want, omit the sauce and serve with Pan-Fried Catfish (page 78).

3 cups all-purpose flour

3 cups white cornmeal

3 tablespoons sugar

1 teaspoon baking powder

1 teaspoon salt

1⅓ cups milk

1 cup water

⅓ cup vegetable oil

1 large egg, beaten

7 to 9 cups corn oil, to fry

Vietnamese-Style Dipping Sauce (see below), to serve

Sift together the flour, cornmeal, sugar, baking powder, and salt in a large bowl. Stir in the milk, water, vegetable oil, and egg just until blended. (The batter will be thick.)

Preheat the oven to 200F (95C). Pour the corn oil into a medium (4- to 6 quart) cast-iron Dutch oven to a depth of 3 inches. Heat the oil over medium high heat until a deep-fry thermometer registers 375F (190C).

Scoop up a heaping tablespoon of the batter and, using another tablespoon, roll the batter twice back and forth between the spoons to form a round fritter. Drop the fritter, using the second tablespoon to help release it, into the oil. Or use a small sorbet scoop, which will hold about 1½ tablespoons of batter.

Fry the hushpuppies in batches (do not crowd the Dutch oven), turning them in the oil often, until golden brown and the exterior is crispy and the interior is cakelike, 1 to 3 minutes total.

Using a slotted spoon, transfer the hushpuppies to a paper towel-lined plate to drain, then to a baking sheet lined with foil and hold in the warm oven until all the batches are ready. Use a slotted spoon to skim the surface of the oil in between batches to keep it clean. Serve at once with Vietnamese-Style Dipping Sauce.

VIETNAMESE-STYLE DIPPING SAUCE

ASIAN FISH SAUCE IS ONE of those ingredients that is an acquired flavor; either you love it or you hate it. It is available at Asian markets.

¾ **cup Asian fish sauce, such as** *nuoc mam* **or** *nam pla*

½ **cup distilled white vinegar**

¼ **cup fresh lime juice**

2 **tablespoons firmly packed light brown sugar**

3 **cloves garlic, crushed through a garlic press**

¼ **cup minced fresh cilantro**

Whisk together all the ingredients in a small glass bowl until well blended. Serve at room temperature soon after preparing it.

BISCUITS

THERE'S NOTHING LIKE A PIPING-HOT biscuit served with plenty of farm-fresh butter and golden honey. What makes a "great" biscuit is very subjective, and there are many passionate arguments about the choice of ingredients and techniques, especially among Southerners. But one thing is agreed upon: You must use Southern soft-wheat flour. When you cut in the shortening, do not attempt to crush all the lumps; leave some behind because they help create flakiness in the finished biscuits. And use a light touch when rolling out the dough.

You can use self-rising flour and omit the baking powder, baking soda, and salt.

Southern flour is becoming more readily available nationwide, and is oftentimes available in gourmet stores in cosmopolitan cities.

> 4 to 4¼ cups all-purpose flour (preferably flour made from soft wheat, such as White Lily, Martha White, Southern Biscuit, or Weisenberger's)
>
> 2 tablespoons baking powder
>
> 1 teaspoon baking soda
>
> 1 teaspoon salt
>
> ⅔ cup solid vegetable shortening, chilled
>
> 1½ cups buttermilk
>
> 4 tablespoons (½ stick) unsalted butter, melted

Preheat the oven to 450F (230C). Sift the flour, baking powder, baking soda, and salt into a large bowl. Cut in the shortening with a pastry blender or fork until mixture resembles coarse crumbs.

Add the buttermilk all at once and immediately stir with a fork until the dough gathers together, adding more buttermilk if necessary to form a soft but not sticky dough.

Knead very briefly on a lightly floured work surface just until smooth. Roll out dough to ¾-inch thickness.

Cut out biscuits with a round 3-inch-diameter cutter, dipping cutter into flour between cuts and tapping off any excess flour. For straight-sided, evenly shaped biscuits, press the cutter straight down, pushing firmly through the dough without twisting. (Twisting the cutter causes biscuits to be uneven.) Re-roll the scraps and repeat the process. You will have about 9 biscuits.

Place biscuits, with sides touching, in an ungreased 12-inch cast-iron skillet. Brush the biscuit tops with the melted butter.

Bake in the center of the oven for 10 minutes; reduce the temperature to 425F (220C) and bake for 10 to 15 minutes or until the biscuits are a rich golden brown on the top and well risen. Serve at once.

CRANBERRY-ORANGE OAT SCONES WITH CRYSTALLIZED GINGER

Makes 8 (3-inch) scones

CRYSTALLIZED GINGER ADDS A DISTINCTIVE flavor to these scones; it is available in well-stocked supermarkets and gourmet stores, as are the dried cranberries.

1 tablespoon unsalted butter, to grease

1½ cups all-purpose flour

½ cup old-fashioned (not instant) oatmeal

2 teaspoons baking powder

1 tablespoon sugar

½ teaspoon salt

2 teaspoons freshly grated orange zest

4 tablespoons (½ stick) unsalted butter, diced and chilled

1 large egg

1 cup heavy cream, plus 1 tablespoon

¾ cup dried cranberries

¼ cup finely chopped crystallized ginger

Adjust oven rack to top third position and preheat the oven to 400F (205C). Grease a large (12- to 14-inch) cast-iron skillet with the 1 tablespoon butter.

Combine the flour, oatmeal, baking powder, sugar, salt, and orange zest in a large bowl and stir, using a fork, until well combined. Using a pastry blender or fork, cut in the butter until the mixture resembles very coarse cornmeal (pea-sized pieces).

Whisk together the egg and 1 cup cream in a medium bowl until well blended and stir in the cranberries and ginger. Pour the liquid mixture over dry ingredients and fold in using a rubber spatula just until combined; do not overmix.

Turn out onto a well-floured work surface and place a large piece of plastic wrap over the dough. Roll dough to ½-inch thickness and remove plastic wrap.

Cut out rounds with a 3-inch floured cutter. Re-roll dough scraps and cut. Transfer rounds to prepared skillet, placing the scones, with sides touching, in a circle in the skillet, with 1 or 2 in the center of the circle. Brush the tops with the 1 tablespoon cream.

Bake for 20 to 25 minutes or until the tops are pale golden brown and a toothpick comes out clean when inserted in the center of a scone. Serve warm.

SAUSAGE WHEELS

Makes 2 dozen

A FAST AND EASY TASTY tidbit that makes use of refrigerated dough (usually in the refrigerated dairy case at the supermarket), these Sausage Wheels are great with soup or as a snack to just pop in your mouth.

1 (8-ounce) can refrigerated crescent-style dinner rolls

2 tablespoons Dijon mustard

12 small country-style sausage links, cooked according to package directions and cooled to room temperature (12 ounces total)

Preheat the oven to 350F (175C). Unroll the crescent roll dough onto a work surface. Using your fingers, firmly pinch the diagonal perforations to seal, and separate each dough sheet at the vertical perforations and then the horizontal perforations to make 4 rectangles.

Arrange the dough rectangles on a work surface so the long side of each is facing you. Cut each rectangle, from a long side, into thirds, so you have a total of 12 pieces.

Divide the mustard among the dough pieces and spread evenly over the top of each. Place a sausage in the lower half just below the center of each and roll up. (The sausage ends will be exposed.) Using a serrated knife in a sawing motion, cut each roll in half, transfer to an ungreased large (12- to 14-inch) cast-iron skillet, and place each slice, seam side down, ½ inch apart.

Bake for 12 to 15 minutes or until the crust is puffed, crisp, and golden brown. Remove from the skillet, let stand for 5 minutes on a wire rack, and serve warm.

SKILLET CORNBREAD

Makes 6 servings

CORNBREAD PURISTS WILL BE UPSET with this colorful confetti cornbread, but they will be pleased with the fact that cast iron provides an outstanding, crisp, golden-brown crust, and in the South, a cast-iron skillet is the only way to bake cornbread. Some folks invert the bread so the crisp crust (from the bottom of the skillet) is on top. Or you can serve it directly from the skillet.

I like to serve it with butter and jalapeño jelly, which is frequently available in supermarkets or gourmet stores.

2 teaspoons bacon drippings or vegetable oil, to grease

1½ cups yellow cornmeal

½ cup all-purpose flour

2 large eggs, beaten

¼ cup vegetable oil

1 cup sour cream

½ cup canned cream-style corn

1 cup shredded sharp cheddar cheese

½ cup drained diced pimientos (available at supermarkets)

¼ cup very thinly sliced scallions (green parts only)

½ teaspoon baking powder

½ teaspoon baking soda

Liberally grease the bottom and sides of a 10-inch cast-iron skillet with the bacon drippings. Place the skillet in a cold oven and preheat the oven to 400F (205C).

Meanwhile, combine all of the ingredients in a large bowl except the baking powder and baking soda, and using a fork, stir together until well blended.

When the oven is hot and just before baking, stir the baking powder and baking soda into the batter until blended. Pour the batter all at once into the hot skillet and smooth the surface.

Bake in the center of the oven for 15 to 20 minutes or until the top is crisp and a toothpick inserted in the center comes out almost clean with a few moist crumbs clinging to it. (The top may not brown.)

Run a small, sharp knife between the edge of the cornbread and the skillet to help loosen the bread. Let stand in the skillet on a wire rack for 5 minutes before serving. Cut into wedges and serve warm directly from the skillet.

CORN STICKS

Makes 12 corn sticks

VERY LUCKY INDIVIDUALS ARE GIVEN heirloom cast-iron corn stick pans. For those who aren't fortunate enough to inherit them, new ones are available.

1 cup all-purpose flour
1 cup yellow cornmeal
1½ teaspoons baking powder
¾ teaspoon salt
2 teaspoons sugar
1 large egg, at room temperature
1 cup milk, at room temperature
2 tablespoons bacon drippings or vegetable oil

Preheat the oven to 425F (220C). Generously coat 2 cast-iron corn stick pans (6 or 7 wells each pan) with nonstick cooking spray, set on a baking sheet, and place in the oven to heat while preparing the batter.

In a medium bowl, stir together the flour, cornmeal, baking powder, salt, and sugar until well blended. In a small bowl, whisk together the egg, milk, and bacon drippings until well blended.

Make a well in the center of the dry ingredients. Pour in the egg mixture and stir just until well blended but do not overmix. (Mixture will be slightly lumpy.)

Spoon some batter into each corn stick well of the hot pans, filling each until level with the rim.

Bake in the center of the oven for 15 to 20 minutes or until the corn sticks spring back when pressed lightly in the centers.

Let cool in the pans on a wire rack for 5 minutes, then remove by prying loose with a fork and inverting the pans. Serve at once.

BROCCOLI AND CHEESE CORNBREAD MUFFINS

Makes 14 to 16 muffins

I RECENTLY WAS INVITED TO a buffet luncheon where the hostess served muffins similar to these. When I asked her where she came up with such a clever muffin idea, she said she found a recipe in the cookbook *Desperation Dinners* by Beverly Mills and Alicia Ross. I was so taken by them that I created this version, which is a loose adaptation. These must be served warm so the cheese oozes. They are terrific with a bowl of tomato or vegetable-beef soup. Also tuck them into your breadbasket the next time you serve roast turkey or beef.

1 cup yellow cornmeal

1 cup all-purpose flour

1 tablespoon baking powder

½ teaspoon salt

1 cup milk

1 large egg, beaten

1 (10-ounce) package frozen chopped broccoli, cooked according to package directions, drained, and cooled to room temperature

8 ounces sharp cheddar cheese, shredded (about 3½ cups)

Preheat the oven to 425F (220C). Line 2 12-cup cast-iron muffin pans with fluted paper cupcake liners.

Using a fork, stir together the cornmeal, flour, baking powder, and salt in a large bowl until well blended. Stir together the milk and egg in a medium bowl until well blended. Add to the cornmeal mixture and stir just until moistened. Stir in the broccoli and cheese just until blended. Do not overmix or the muffins will be tough. Spoon the batter into the pans, filling the cups three-quarters full. Fill any unused cups halfway with water.

Bake 10 to 15 minutes or until the muffins just begin to brown around the edges and spring back when lightly pressed.

Let the muffins cool in the pans on a wire rack for 5 minutes. Run a small, sharp knife around each cup to help loosen the muffins from the pans, and serve warm.

NATIVE AMERICAN PIÑON PANCAKES WITH MAPLE SYRUP

Makes 4 servings

SERVE THESE BREAKFAST DELIGHTS ALONGSIDE the Sunday paper. These lovely pancakes unite the favors of pine nuts and maple and are delectable. Because they are crêpelike in size and thinness, they can also be filled with your choice of complementary filling, rolled up, and served as an appetizer for a formal dinner (omit the maple syrup, of course). Pine nuts are available at Italian grocery stores, gourmet shops, and most supermarkets.

2 cups all-purpose flour

1 teaspoon salt

4 large eggs

2 cups milk

4 tablespoons (½ stick) unsalted butter, melted

1 cup pine nuts (also called *pignoli*)

Vegetable oil, as needed

Maple syrup, heated, to serve

Melted unsalted butter, to serve

Combine the flour, salt, eggs, milk, and butter in a large bowl and whisk until well blended and smooth. Cover and refrigerate for 30 minutes.

Meanwhile, add the pine nuts to a large (12- to 14-inch) cast-iron skillet or griddle over medium heat and dry-toast the pine nuts, tossing, until golden brown, 4 to 6 minutes. Remove from the skillet, let cool, and reserve.

Preheat the oven to 200F (95C). Place the skillet over medium heat, and heat 1 tablespoon oil for 2 minutes. Drop 3 tablespoons of batter per pancake in the skillet. Sprinkle each pancake evenly with 2 teaspoons pine nuts. When bubbles form on the surface, 1 to 2 minutes, flip each pancake over and cook until lightly browned on both sides. Hold the pancakes in the warm oven while cooking remaining batter.

Repeat the process, heating more oil in between batches as needed, until all the batter and pine nuts have been used. Serve at once with the maple syrup and melted butter.

BUTTERMILK-LEMON FLAPJACKS
WITH STRAWBERRY SAUCE

Makes 12 to 14 pancakes

THESE FLAPJACKS HAVE A PRETTY, light-yellow color from the buttermilk and a faint but certain lemony taste. The flapjacks by themselves are not especially sweet, because the sauce provides the natural, overall sweetness to this recipe.

SAUCE

>   1 pound ripe fresh strawberries, thinly sliced
>
>   ½ cup confectioners' sugar

PANCAKES

>   3 large eggs, separated
>
>   3 tablespoons sugar
>
>   2 cups buttermilk
>
>   ¼ cup (½ stick) unsalted butter, melted
>
>   2 cups all-purpose flour
>
>   1 teaspoon baking soda
>
>   2½ teaspoons freshly grated lemon zest
>
>   ¼ teaspoon lemon extract
>
>   Vegetable oil, to grease

TO PREPARE THE SAUCE: Stir together the strawberries and confectioners' sugar in a medium glass or stainless steel bowl until well blended. Cover and reserve until ready to use.

TO MAKE THE PANCAKES: In a large bowl, beat the egg yolks with the sugar with an electric mixer on medium-high speed until pale yellow, about 1 minute. Beat in the buttermilk, butter, flour, baking soda, lemon zest, and lemon extract until well blended.

Working quickly, in a medium bowl, beat the egg whites with an electric mixer on medium-high speed until stiff, glossy (but not dry) peaks form, and the peaks hold their shape when the beaters are raised upside down, about 2 minutes. Fold the beaten egg whites into the batter just until combined and no white streaks remain.

Preheat the oven to 200F (95C). Brush a cast-iron griddle generously with some of the oil and heat for 2 minutes over medium-high heat or until hot enough to make drops of water dance over the surface.

Working in batches, pour about ⅓ cup of batter for each pancake onto the griddle, forming 4-inch rounds. Cook pancakes until the undersides are golden and the tops are bubbly, 1 to 2 minutes. Flip the pancakes over and lightly brown on the other side, about 1 minute. Brush the griddle lightly with oil between batches, and hold the pancakes on a baking sheet in the warm oven while preparing the remaining pancakes. Serve at once with the sauce.

RED RASPBERRY
FRENCH TOAST POCKETS

Makes 4 servings (3 pieces each)

YES! JUST LIKE THE TITLE—French toast with a pocket—a pocket full of raspberries! Or you can substitute a fruit combination, perhaps strawberries and bananas. If your local bakery or supermarket doesn't sell challah bread, choose another sweet, soft-crusted bread with a fluffy interior that can be cut easily into "pockets."

6 (1½-inch-thick) diagonal slices challah or other sweet white bread

2 cups ripe fresh raspberries

6 large eggs

1 cup milk

2 teaspoons pure vanilla extract

4 tablespoons (½ stick) unsalted butter

¼ cup confectioners' sugar, to serve

¼ teaspoon ground cinnamon, to serve

¼ teaspoon ground nutmeg, to serve

Maple syrup, heated, to serve

Using kitchen scissors, cut a "pocket" 2 inches deep into the cut edge of each slice (but not all the way through to the crust).

Using your fingers, fill each bread slice with one-sixth of the raspberries. In a deep, medium bowl, whisk together the eggs, milk, and vanilla until well blended.

Preheat the oven to 200F (95C). Melt 2 tablespoons of the butter in a large (12- to 14-inch) cast-iron skillet or cast-iron griddle over medium heat until it is very hot but not smoking, about 30 seconds.

Working quickly, using your fingers, briefly dip the bread (pinching each pocket closed while you do so, so as not to spill out the raspberries) in the egg mixture to coat. Add to the skillet.

Fry the French toast in batches of 3 (do not crowd the skillet) until the surface lightly browns on each side, turning over the slices carefully, 2 to 3 minutes. Transfer to a baking sheet and hold in the warm oven until ready to serve. Melt the remaining 2 tablespoons butter in the skillet before adding the second batch.

Stir together the confectioners' sugar, cinnamon, and nutmeg until well blended and transfer to a sieve. Using the sieve, dust the mixture over the French toast pockets and serve at once with a pitcher of warm maple syrup.

APPLE CLAFOUTI

THIS LIGHT AND AIRY LARGE breakfast pancake deflates rather quickly once removed from the oven, so be prepared to serve it immediately.

CLAFOUTI

> 3 large eggs
>
> 1 large egg white
>
> 1 cup milk
>
> ⅔ cup all-purpose flour
>
> 2 tablespoons sugar
>
> 2 tablespoons unsalted butter, to grease

TOPPING

> 2 medium Granny Smith apples, unpeeled, cut into ¼-inch cubes
>
> ⅓ cup firmly packed light brown sugar
>
> 3 tablespoons unsalted butter, melted
>
> ¼ cup raisins
>
> 1 teaspoon ground cinnamon
>
> ¼ teaspoon ground nutmeg

Preheat the oven to 425F (220C). To make the clafouti: In a large bowl, beat together all the ingredients except the butter with an electric mixer on medium speed just until well blended and smooth, 2 minutes.

Add the butter to a 12-inch cast-iron skillet. Place the skillet on the center oven rack and melt the butter, about 1 minute.

Remove the skillet from the oven and tilt to coat the bottom and sides with the melted butter. Working quickly, pour in the batter. Bake on the center rack for 15 to 20 minutes or until puffed and the edges are lightly golden brown.

MEANWHILE, PREPARE THE TOPPING: In a small bowl, stir together all the ingredients until well blended.

Spread the clafouti with the apple topping and serve at once, directly from the skillet.

FANCIFUL CHIVE POPOVERS

Makes 8 to 12 (depending on the number and size of cups in the popover pan)

ZIPPY SNIPPETS OF FRESH CHIVES impart their flavor to my rendition of one of my all-time favorite (and albeit whimsical) foodstuffs—popovers.

- **2 large eggs, beaten, at room temperature**
- **1 cup milk, at room temperature**
- **2 tablespoons unsalted butter, melted**
- **1 cup all-purpose flour**
- **½ teaspoon salt**
- **¼ teaspoon freshly ground pepper**
- **¼ cup very thinly sliced or snipped fresh chives**

Coat the cups of a cast-iron popover pan or a cast-iron muffin pan with nonstick cooking spray. In a medium bowl, combine the eggs, milk, and butter with an electric mixer. Beat on medium speed until blended, about 1 minute. Add the flour, salt, and pepper and beat on medium speed just until blended and smooth, 1 minute. Don't overmix or popovers will be tough. Stir in the chives just until blended.

Pour the batter into the prepared pan, filling the cups ⅔ full. Fill any unused cups halfway with water.

Place on a baking sheet and transfer to a cold oven (not preheated) and set temperature at 425F (220C). Bake for 20 to 30 minutes (depending on the size of the cups in the popover pan), or until the popovers are puffed, crisp, and golden brown.

Remove the popovers from the oven and run a small, sharp knife around each cup to help loosen the popovers from the pan. Serve at once.

GREAT GARLIC BREAD

A GENEROUS DOSE OF GARLIC permeates my version of this addictive garlic bread that also includes Parmesan cheese. It is lent a rustic look when served in a cast-iron skillet. Extra-virgin olive oil is available from gourmet stores and most supermarkets.

2 tablespoons extra-virgin olive oil

7 cloves garlic, crushed through a garlic press

¼ cup (½ stick) unsalted butter, at room temperature

1 teaspoon garlic salt

2 tablespoons freshly grated Parmesan cheese

2 tablespoons minced fresh parsley

Salt and freshly ground pepper, to taste

1 (1-pound) loaf Italian bread (about 15 inches long)

Preheat the oven to 350F (175C). Combine the oil, garlic, and butter in the bowl of a food processor fitted with a metal blade and process for 2 minutes, scraping down the sides of the bowl as necessary, until the mixture is fairly smooth and pastelike. Stir in the garlic salt, Parmesan cheese, and parsley and stir until well blended. Season with salt and pepper.

Cut the loaf in half crosswise, then cut the halves crosswise on the diagonal at 1-inch intervals, stopping ½ inch from the bottom of the loaf (do not cut all the way through the bread).

Place the loaf halves in a large (12- to 14-inch) cast-iron skillet. Using your fingers, gently spread open the slices, but do not pull them apart. Distribute and spread the garlic mixture evenly among the slices.

Bake in the middle third of the oven for 10 minutes or until the bread is heated through and the crust is crispy. If the crust becomes too brown, tent the bread loosely with foil. Serve at once.

DESSERTS

Banana-Coconut Loaf with Coconut Icing

Coconut Icing

Apricot Pandowdy

Rose Petal Cupcakes with Rose Glaze

Pumpkin Harvest Spice Cake

Bananas Foster

Spiced Caramelized Pear Skillet Cake with Vanilla Whipped Cream

Baked Stuffed Peaches, Piedmont Style

Souffléed Bittersweet Chocolate Omelet with Hot Fudge Sauce

Plum Kuchen

Irresistibly Intense Strawberry Heartcakes

Peach Gingerbread Upside-Down Cake

Fried Peanut-Coated Peanut Butter Ice Cream Balls

Cranberry-Almond Tart

Apple Dessert Dumplings with Cinnamon Ice Cream

Cinnamon Ice Cream

Chocolate Fudge Snack Cake

Chocolate Muffins with Chocolate Cheesecake Topping

Chocolate Lovers' Dessert Pizza

Warm Chocolate Black Bread Pudding

Lemon-Cardamom Cake

Blueberry Buckle with Almond Crumb Topping

Wild Blackberry Cobbler

Strawberry Cream Stack Cake

Mincemeat Turnovers

BANANA-COCONUT LOAF
WITH COCONUT ICING

FOR OPTIMUM BANANA FLAVOR, MAKE sure you use bananas that are very ripe. The cream of coconut (available from supermarkets or liquor stores) adds extra moistness to the cake (it is also used in the icing). It is not mandatory to ice this cake, but the homey tan-colored icing (from the light brown sugar) only adds to its appeal.

1½ cups cake flour

½ teaspoon baking soda

½ teaspoon baking powder

¼ teaspoon salt

1 stick (½ cup) unsalted butter, at room temperature

1 cup sugar

2 large eggs

1 teaspoon pure vanilla extract

1 cup mashed very ripe bananas

¼ cup canned cream of coconut, such as Coco López brand

¾ cup shredded sweetened coconut, toasted

¾ cup coarsely chopped macadamia nuts or coarsely chopped walnuts

Confectioners' sugar (optional)

Coconut Icing (see below, optional), to serve

Preheat the oven to 350F (175C). Coat the interior of a 9 × 5-inch cast-iron loaf pan with nonstick cooking spray.

Sift together the flour, baking soda, baking powder, and salt into a medium bowl and set aside.

In a large bowl, beat the butter and sugar with an electric mixer on medium speed until light and fluffy. Beat in the eggs, 1 at a time, just until incorporated. Beat in the vanilla and the bananas just until blended.

On low speed, beat in the flour mixture in thirds, alternating with the cream of coconut just until well blended; do not overmix. Stir in the coconut and macadamia nuts until well distributed.

Spoon into the prepared loaf pan and smooth the surface. Bake on the center oven rack for 50 to 60 minutes or until the top is deep golden brown and a cake tester or toothpick inserted 1 inch from the center comes out almost clean with just a few moist crumbs clinging to it.

Let cool in the pan on a wire rack for 10 minutes. Run a small, sharp knife around the edge to help loosen the cake from pan. Unmold, and using a sieve, dust with the confectioners' sugar, if using, and serve warm. Or let cool completely on the wire rack and frost with the Coconut Icing, if using, and serve at room temperature

COCONUT ICING

Makes about 2 cups

6 tablespoons unsalted butter

1 cup firmly packed light brown sugar

½ cup canned cream of coconut, such as the Coco López brand

3 cups confectioners' sugar, sifted

¼ teaspoon coconut extract (available at most supermarkets and gourmet or baking shops)

Melt the butter in a heavy 2- to 3-quart saucepan over low heat. Stir in the brown sugar and cook, stirring often, until the sugar has dissolved, about 2 minutes.

Increase the heat to medium and bring to a boil, stirring often. Boil until slightly thickened, about 1 minute, stirring constantly.

Remove from the heat and let cool for 5 minutes, then transfer the icing to a medium bowl. Beat the icing with an electric mixer on high speed until completely cool. Beat in the cream of coconut, confectioners' sugar, and coconut extract until well blended and smooth.

APRICOT PANDOWDY

Makes 4 to 6 servings

THERE DOESN'T SEEM TO BE many recipes utilizing fresh, juicy, sensual apricots, and I thought that creating a recipe using the method of "dowdying" them would be an excellent choice. The inception of this term is unknown, but it refers to the process of breaking up pastry crust and pressing it into a fruit mixture.

CRUST

> 1½ cups all-purpose flour
>
> 1 teaspoon sugar
>
> ½ teaspoon salt
>
> 6 tablespoons unsalted butter, cut into ½-inch cubes, chilled
>
> 1½ tablespoons solid vegetable shortening, chilled
>
> 3 to 4 tablespoons chilled water, or as needed

FILLING

> 16 ripe fresh apricots or 2 (15-ounce) cans apricot halves, drained and thinly sliced
>
> 1 cup apricot jam
>
> 1 tablespoon unsalted butter
>
> Vanilla ice cream, to serve

TO PREPARE THE CRUST: Using a fork, stir together the flour, sugar, and salt in a medium bowl until well blended. Using a pastry blender or a fork, cut in the butter and shortening until the mixture resembles coarse crumbs.

Add the water, 1 tablespoon at a time, and toss with a fork just until the dough comes together.

Shape the dough into a disk. Cover with waxed paper, then plastic wrap, and refrigerate for at least 2 hours or preferably overnight before rolling out.

TO MAKE THE FILLING: Preheat the oven to 400F (205C). Liberally grease a 9-inch cast-iron skillet.

In a medium bowl, stir together the sliced apricots and apricot jam until well combined. Spoon the mixture into the prepared skillet and dot with the butter.

On a lightly floured work surface, roll out the dough to a 10-inch round. Place it over the filling, and using a small, sharp knife, trim off the ragged edges so that the pastry is flush with the edges of the skillet. Cut 3 diagonal slashes in the crust to form steam vents.

Bake for 20 to 30 minutes or until the crust is lightly golden. Remove the pandowdy from the oven and cut the crust into 1-inch squares. Using a spatula, press the squares down into the apricot filling so the pastry is submerged.

Reduce the oven temperature to 350F (175C). Return the pandowdy to the oven and bake for 20 to 30 minutes more or until bubbling and the crust is a delicate golden brown. Serve warm in shallow bowls with ice cream.

ROSE PETAL CUPCAKES
WITH ROSE GLAZE

Makes about 1 dozen

WHEN FOLKS THINK OF "CAST IRON," they tend to think of rugged cookware, and rustic, hearty foods, which is why I felt it important to include a recipe that proves that delicate foods can be baked in cast iron, too. These cupcakes are charming with their blush of pink glaze and belong on a tea table, where only ladies wearing white gloves are befit to partake of them. These dainties have the floral, exotic flavor of roses because of the edible rose water used. Have you ever been so overcome with the fabulous fragrance of a rose that as you inhaled it in, you thought it smelled so good you wanted to eat it? Well, here's your chance. This dessert was inspired by a recipe for Rose Petal Bread in *All the Best Muffins and Quick Breads* by Joie Warner. Rose water has been a popular flavoring for centuries in Middle Eastern, Indian, and Chinese cuisines, and I think that it is one of the ingredients that you'll be seeing more of in the United States in the near future.

CUPCAKES

2 cups all-purpose flour

2 teaspoons baking powder

½ teaspoon salt

1 stick (½ cup) unsalted butter, at room temperature

¾ cup sugar

2 large eggs

1 cup milk

2 teaspoons rose water (available from gourmet shops or ethnic markets)

½ cup organic pesticide-free red rose petals (Using kitchen scissors, trim away and discard the white part and cut each petal into quarters.)

GLAZE

1 cup confectioners' sugar

1 to 2 tablespoons heavy cream

½ teaspoon rose water

1 drop red food coloring

Candied rose petals, to garnish (optional, available at gourmet shops)

To make the cupcakes: Preheat the oven to 350F (175C). Place a fluted paper cupcake liner in each of the 12 cups of a cast-iron muffin pan.

Sift together the flour, baking powder, and salt into a large bowl.

In a large bowl, beat the butter and sugar with an electric mixer on medium speed until light and fluffy, 3 minutes. Beat in the eggs, 1 at a time, then the milk and rose water until well blended.

Add the dry ingredients and beat on low speed, just until combined, being careful not to overmix. Working quickly, fold in the rose petals until blended.

Spoon the batter into the prepared muffin cups, filling the cups three-quarters full, and smooth the surface. Fill any unused cups halfway with water.

Bake on the center oven rack for 15 to 20 minutes or until a cake tester or toothpick inserted in the center comes out almost clean with a few moist crumbs clinging to it.

Remove from the oven and let the cupcakes cool in the pan on a wire rack for 5 minutes. Turn the cupcakes out onto the wire rack and let cool completely. Remove cupcakes from the paper liners.

Meanwhile, make the glaze: In a small bowl, stir together the confectioners' sugar and enough cream to form a smooth, medium thin glaze. Stir in the rose water and red food coloring until well blended; the glaze should be colored a light pink.

Place the cupcakes on a wire rack set over waxed paper. Spread the glaze over the top of cupcakes, allowing the glaze to drip over the sides, and wipe off any excess. Place a candied rose in the center of each, if desired. Let stand at room temperature until the glaze sets, about 30 minutes, before serving.

PUMPKIN HARVEST SPICE CAKE

Makes 1 (9 × 5-inch) loaf; 6 servings

THIS LOAF-SHAPED QUICK CAKE HAS a warming aftertaste of clove, while the buttermilk adds richness. I like to eat this cake plain and unadorned, but for guests, I have served slices slathered with cream cheese, and during the fall, when pumpkin ice cream is available, I've even added a scoop on the side.

1½ cups all-purpose flour

¾ teaspoon baking powder

½ teaspoon baking soda

¼ teaspoon salt

½ teaspoon ground cinnamon

¼ teaspoon ground nutmeg

¼ teaspoon ground ginger

¼ teaspoon ground cloves

1 large egg

1 large egg white

6 tablespoons sugar

¼ cup firmly packed light brown sugar

1 cup firmly packed canned pumpkin

6 tablespoons buttermilk

1½ tablespoons vegetable oil

1 teaspoon pure vanilla extract

Confectioners' sugar, to dust

Preheat the oven to 350F (175C). Coat a 9 × 5-inch cast-iron loaf pan with vegetable spray.

Sift together the flour, baking powder, baking soda, salt, and spices in a large bowl.

In a medium bowl, using a fork, stir together the egg, egg white, granulated sugar, brown sugar, pumpkin, buttermilk, oil, and vanilla and stir vigorously until well blended and smooth.

Stir into the reserved flour mixture just until well blended and smooth; do not overmix. Pour the batter into the prepared loaf pan and smooth the surface.

Bake on the center oven rack for 30 to 35 minutes, or until a cake tester or toothpick inserted 1 inch from the center comes out almost clean with a few moist crumbs clinging to it.

Cool in the pan on a wire rack for 15 minutes. Unmold the cake onto the rack and let cool to room temperature. Once the cake is cool, sift confectioners' sugar over the top and serve.

BANANAS FOSTER

Makes 4 servings

RATHER THAN A CHAFING DISH, a cast-iron skillet works nicely for this flamboyant dish since cast iron retains heat so well. You will need to use a gas range, not electric, for the flambé technique. Please do be careful and take the precautions given below to make flambéing safe in your home kitchen.

4 small ripe bananas

Juice of ½ lemon

6 tablespoons unsalted butter

⅔ cup firmly packed light brown sugar

¼ cup banana liqueur

½ teaspoon ground cinnamon

3 tablespoons light rum

Vanilla ice cream, to serve

Peel the bananas. Cut in half crosswise, then lengthwise, and brush with the lemon juice.

In a medium (10- to 12-inch) cast-iron skillet over medium heat, melt the butter. Stir in the brown sugar and cook, stirring, until the sugar has dissolved, 2 minutes. Stir in the banana liqueur and cinnamon until well blended.

Add the bananas, cut side down, and cook, turning over once with tongs, just until the bananas are well coated and hot (not browned), 4 minutes. Remove the skillet from the heat.

Pour the rum into a 2- to 3-quart saucepan over low heat. Let heat for 1 minute. Remove the saucepan from the heat. Wearing long, flameproof oven mitts, and using a long fireplace match, very carefully light the rum at the side, then very carefully pour over the bananas in the skillet, not moving the skillet, but letting it stand until the flames quickly die out. Serve at once over vanilla ice cream.

Spiced Caramelized Pear Skillet Cake with Vanilla Whipped Cream

Makes 4 to 6 servings

THIS THIN, RICH CAKE REMINDS me of the French *tarte tatin,* but instead of caramelized apples, it's topped with caramelized pears. It may seem that simple, unappreciated fruit couldn't become a sinful dessert, but this dessert is. For even more excess, serve it with Häagen-Daz's Dulce de Leche ice cream (caramel ice cream with caramel swirl).

1¼ cups sugar

⅓ cup water

3 medium fresh Bartlett pears (about 1 pound)

Juice of 1 lemon

1 cup all-purpose flour

2 teaspoons baking powder

¼ teaspoon salt

¼ teaspoon ground ginger

¼ teaspoon ground nutmeg

¼ teaspoon ground cinnamon

2 large egg yolks

2 tablespoons butter, melted and cooled

¼ cup milk

½ teaspoon pure vanilla extract

VANILLA WHIPPED CREAM

1 cup heavy cream

3 tablespoons confectioners' sugar

½ teaspoon pure vanilla extract

Preheat the oven to 350F (175C). Liberally coat the interior of a 10-inch cast-iron skillet with nonstick cooking spray.

Place ¾ cup of the sugar and the water in a 1½- to 2-quart saucepan and stir until well blended. Set over medium heat and bring to a boil, without stirring. Reduce the heat to low and simmer, without stirring, until the syrup just turns caramel, 10 to 15 minutes. Working quickly, remove the saucepan from the heat and immediately pour the caramel syrup into the prepared skillet. Tilt the skillet around to coat the bottom and sides with the caramel and place on a baking sheet.

Peel the pears and cut into ½-inch cubes. As you cut the pears, gently toss them with the lemon juice in a small bowl until well blended and well coated with the lemon juice. Reserve until ready to use.

Sift together the flour, baking powder, salt, and spices in a medium bowl and reserve.

Place the egg yolks and remaining ½ cup sugar in a bowl. With an electric mixer, beat on medium speed until the sugar is dissolved, 2 minutes. Beat in the butter, milk, and vanilla until well blended.

Strain the reserved pear mixture and gently stir into the batter (so as not to break the pears) until well blended.

Ladle the batter over the caramel in the skillet and smooth the surface. Bake on the center oven rack for 25 to 35 minutes, or until a cake tester or toothpick inserted 1 inch from the center comes out almost clean with a few moist crumbs clinging to it.

MEANWHILE, PREPARE THE WHIPPED CREAM: In a chilled medium bowl, whip the cream, confectioners' sugar, and vanilla until stiff peaks form. Cover and chill until ready to serve.

Cool the cake in the skillet on a wire rack for 5 minutes. Run a small, sharp knife around the cake edge to loosen the sides from the skillet, then invert the cake onto a serving platter. If any pears stick to the bottom of the skillet, transfer them to the top of the cake with the tip of a knife. If any caramel sticks to the bottom of the skillet, scrape it out and drizzle it onto the cake. Serve warm with a dollop of the whipped cream.

BAKED STUFFED PEACHES, PIEDMONT STYLE

Makes 6 servings

THIS LUSCIOUS SEASONAL DESSERT CAN be prepared with nectarines as well. Choose fruit that is ripe but not too soft. It is a classic Italian dessert from the Piedmont where peaches grow abundantly. The filling is made of amarettini (or called amaretti, if the cookies are larger), which are crisp almond-scented macaroon cookies flavored with a bitter almond paste or apricot kernel paste available from Italian groceries or gourmet stores.

3 tablespoons unsalted butter

1 (1.41 ounce) box Amarettini di Saronno

3 tablespoons sugar

1 large egg, beaten

3 large fresh ripe peaches (about 1½ pounds)

¼ cup dry Marsala (an Italian fortified wine)

6 sprigs fresh mint, to garnish

Preheat the oven to 375F (190C). Liberally grease a 9-inch cast-iron skillet with 1 tablespoon of the butter.

Place the amarettini in a food processor fitted with the metal blade and pulse into small crumbs (you should have about ½ cup crumbs). Or place them into a resealable plastic bag, seal, and crush with a rolling pin or mallet into small crumbs.

Combine the crumbs and sugar in a medium bowl. Stir in the beaten egg slowly, a little at a time, adding enough egg so that the mixture just holds together; don't allow the mixture to get so wet it doesn't hold its shape.

Working over a large bowl to catch any juice, cut the peaches in half around the midline and remove and discard the pits. Place the peach halves close to one another in the prepared skillet, cut side up. Spoon one-sixth of the crumb mixture into each peach cavity, pressing firmly with your fingers to compact the filling.

Dot the tops with the remaining 2 tablespoons butter. Pour the Marsala and any peach juice left in the bowl around the peaches in the skillet.

Bake for 30 minutes or until the peaches are soft but still hold their shape and the filling surface is crisp and begins to brown.

Spoon a small pool of the cooking juices on each small dessert plate, then place a peach half, filling side up, on top of juice. Garnish with a fresh mint sprig and serve.

Souffléed Bittersweet Chocolate Omelet with Hot Fudge Sauce

Makes 2 to 4 servings; 3 cups sauce

MAKE THIS HOMEMADE HOT FUDGE sauce, or substitute store-bought chocolate sauce, and heat it before serving. Any leftover homemade sauce can be stored in an airtight container in the refrigerator for 3 months or frozen for 6 months.

HOT FUDGE SAUCE
> 1 cup canned evaporated milk
>
> 2 cups sugar
>
> ¼ teaspoon salt
>
> ¼ cup light corn syrup
>
> 6 tablespoons unsalted butter
>
> 4 ounces unsweetened chocolate
>
> 2 ounces semisweet chocolate
>
> 2½ teaspoons pure vanilla extract

OMELET
> 1 tablespoon unsalted butter, to grease
>
> 6 tablespoons sugar
>
> 1 tablespoon unsweetened cocoa powder
>
> 4 large eggs, separated
>
> Pinch salt
>
> ¼ teaspoon cream of tartar
>
> 2 ounces semisweet chocolate, melted and cooled

TO PREPARE THE FUDGE SAUCE: Combine the evaporated milk, sugar, salt, corn syrup, butter, and chocolates in the upper pan of a double boiler. Partially fill the bottom pan with simmering water and place over medium heat.

Heat the chocolate mixture, stirring, until the butter and chocolate have melted. Cook, stirring often, until it is smooth and slightly thickened, about 10 minutes. Stir in the vanilla. Remove the top pan from the bottom and cover to keep warm until ready to serve.

TO MAKE THE OMELET: Preheat the oven to 375F (190C). Liberally grease the bottom and sides of a 10-inch cast-iron skillet with the butter. Combine 1 tablespoon of the sugar and the cocoa powder in a small fine-meshed sieve and sift the mixture over the bottom and sides of the skillet until evenly dusted and set aside.

In a large bowl, beat the egg whites with an electric mixer on medium-high speed until foamy, about 2 minutes. Add the salt and cream of tartar, reduce the speed to medium, and beat until soft peaks form, about 1 minute. Increase speed to medium-high and beat in 2 tablespoons of the sugar until stiff, glossy (but not dry) peaks form, and the peaks hold their shape when the beaters are turned upside down, about 2 minutes. Set aside.

In a medium bowl, beat the egg yolks with an electric mixer on medium speed until thick and pale in color, about 1 minute. Beat in the remaining 3 tablespoons sugar until well blended.

Working quickly, stir the chocolate into the egg yolk mixture. Fold in the beaten egg whites. Spoon into the prepared skillet and smooth the surface.

Bake on the center oven rack for 15 minutes or until puffy and set. Working quickly, drizzle a pool of the hot sauce on each serving plate, top with a wedge of the omelet, and drizzle with some more sauce. Serve at once.

PLUM KUCHEN

Makes 6 servings

OFTENTIMES KUCHEN, A GERMAN COFFEECAKE, is made with yeast. My translation skips the yeast and proffers a charming, medium-thick, homespun skillet cake.

1 tablespoon butter, to grease

1 tablespoon all-purpose flour, to dust

1½ cups all-purpose flour

1½ teaspoons baking powder

1½ teaspoons ground cinnamon, divided

1¼ cups firmly packed dark-brown sugar, divided

1 stick (½ cup) unsalted butter, cut into ½-inch cubes and chilled

2 large eggs

½ cup milk

8 medium-sized fresh purple plums (1¼ pounds total)

Preheat the oven to 350F (175C). Liberally grease the bottom and sides of a 10-inch cast-iron skillet with the 1 tablespoon butter and dust it with the 1 tablespoon flour, gently shaking the skillet to remove any excess flour.

Sift together the 1½ cups flour, baking powder, and ½ teaspoon of the cinnamon in a large bowl. Stir in 1 cup of the brown sugar until well blended. Using a pastry blender or fork, cut in the ½ cup butter until the mixture resembles coarse crumbs. Transfer 2 tablespoons of this mixture to a small bowl, along with the remaining ¼ cup brown sugar and the remaining 1 teaspoon cinnamon, and stir until well blended (this mixture forms the topping).

In a medium bowl, whisk the eggs and milk until well blended. Stir egg mixture into the flour mixture just until blended; do not overmix. Pour batter evenly into the prepared skillet and smooth the surface.

Working over a large bowl to catch any juice, cut the plums in half around the midline and remove and discard the pits. Arrange the plum halves, cut side down, on top of the batter in a decorative pattern, and drizzle any juice left behind in the bowl over them. Sprinkle the topping over all.

Bake on the center oven rack for 40 to 50 minutes or until a cake tester or toothpick inserted 1 inch from the center comes out almost clean with a few moist crumbs clinging to it. Cut into wedges and serve hot directly from the skillet.

IRRESISTIBLY INTENSE
STRAWBERRY HEARTCAKES

Makes 9 servings

THE PROFILE OF A STRAWBERRY has always impressed me because it's reminiscent of a heart. The color of fresh strawberries is so magnificent it seemed only appropriate that I create heart-shaped shortcakes to echo this theme.

> **Biscuits (page 170)**
> **2 pounds fresh strawberries**
> **1 tablespoon Grand Marnier or other orange liqueur**
> **⅓ cup confectioners' sugar**
> **Vanilla Whipped Cream (page 195)**

Make the biscuits according to the recipe, except use a 3-inch heart-shaped cookie cutter to cut the biscuits.

Halve any large berries and transfer to a medium glass or stainless steel bowl. Thinly slice the remaining berries and transfer two-thirds of them to the bowl. Using a fork, lightly crush the remaining one-third of the berries and transfer them along with their juice to the bowl. Add the Grand Marnier and the confectioners' sugar and stir until well blended. Cover and refrigerate until ready to serve.

Just before serving, prepare the Vanilla Whipped Cream.

TO SERVE: Using a serrated knife, cut each cooled biscuit through the middle and split apart. Place bottom layers on individual plates. Spoon slightly more than half the berry mixture and juice over the bottom layers. Place the tops on and spoon the remaining berries over the tops. Dollop with the whipped cream and serve at once.

PEACH GINGERBREAD UPSIDE-DOWN CAKE

Makes 6 servings

GINGERBREAD IS ONE OF MY all-time favorite cakes (but my list of "favorite cakes" is quite lengthy). I even fancy it for breakfast. When paired with peaches, it can't be outdone in the gingerbread category, especially with its Southern flavors. It is so magical to invert a plain, innocent-looking cake to reveal the glistening, vivid peach topping. Once the cake is bottom-side-up and ready for serving, you can top it with a cloud of the Vanilla Whipped Cream (page 195). Because I live in the South, I typically make this with fresh sun-ripened peaches straight from the tree, but I also like it during the wintertime, so I've called for canned peaches here.

TOPPING

6 tablespoons unsalted butter

½ cup firmly packed dark brown sugar

1 tablespoon ginger liqueur, ginger-flavored brandy, or peach brandy

1 (29-ounce) can sliced peaches (packed in heavy syrup), drained

GINGERBREAD

1½ cups all-purpose flour

¾ teaspoon baking soda

¼ teaspoon salt

2 teaspoons ground ginger

1 teaspoon ground cinnamon

¼ teaspoon ground nutmeg

¼ teaspoon ground cloves

1 stick (½ cup) unsalted butter, at room temperature

½ cup firmly packed dark brown sugar

1 large egg, beaten

¼ cup molasses

⅓ cup boiling water

1 teaspoon pure vanilla extract

1 tablespoon ginger liqueur, ginger-flavored brandy, or substitute peach brandy

Vanilla Whipped Cream, (page 194) to serve

Preheat the oven to 350F (175C). To prepare the topping: Melt the butter in a 10-inch cast-iron skillet over low heat. Increase the heat to medium and stir in the brown sugar. Cook, stirring, until the brown sugar is dissolved and the mixture is bubbly, about 2 minutes. Remove the skillet from the heat and stir in the 1 tablespoon of ginger liqueur.

Working quickly, using a fork, place each peach slice on its side, placing them tip-to-tip and side-to-side to form concentric circles on the surface of the topping in the bottom of the skillet.

TO MAKE THE GINGERBREAD: Sift together the flour, baking soda, salt, and spices in a medium bowl and reserve.

In a large bowl, beat together the butter and brown sugar with an electric mixer on low speed until light and fluffy, 1 minute. Add the egg and molasses and beat just until well blended and set aside.

In a small bowl, whisk together the boiling water, vanilla, and ginger liqueur until well blended.

Stir the reserved flour mixture and the boiling water mixture into the reserved butter-sugar mixture, just until blended; do not overmix.

Pour the batter in an even layer over the peaches in the skillet and gently smooth the top, being careful to not move the peaches. Bake on the center rack for 30 to 35 minutes or until a cake tester or toothpick inserted 1 inch from the center comes out almost clean with a few moist crumbs clinging to it.

Cool the cake in the skillet on a wire rack for 5 minutes. Run a small, sharp knife around the cake edge to loosen the sides from the skillet, then invert the cake onto a serving platter. If any peaches stick to the bottom of the skillet, transfer them to the top of the cake with the tip of a knife. If any topping sticks to the bottom of the skillet, scrape it out and drizzle it onto the cake. Serve warm with whipped cream.

FRIED PEANUT-COATED
PEANUT BUTTER ICE CREAM BALLS

Makes 6 servings (1 fried ice cream ball each)

THE STARTLING CONTRAST OF COLD ice cream and hot, crunchy crisp coating is a real palate-pleaser. To me, a crisp, salty-sweet peanut coating seems a natural for peanut butter ice cream, but you can pair it with any ice cream you like. Experiment with combining your favorites; I've used chocolate ice cream coated with crushed chocolate wafers and macadamia nuts. You won't need the full amount of ice cream, but the larger container is much easier to scoop from and it's faster to scoop from a box rather than a tub of the ice cream. Have your bowls and Hot Fudge Sauce ready, because this recipe does need to be served immediately.

I begin this recipe two days before I plan to serve it by coating the ice cream balls with the chopped peanut coating and freezing them, then coating them with the cookie-crumb coating and freezing again. The coated ice cream balls should be frozen rock-hard for the recipe to be a tremendous success. The rewards are well worth the effort of the careful planning.

1 cup finely chopped salted peanuts

½ gallon peanut butter or other ice cream of your choice

2 large eggs

2 cups crushed vanilla wafers (available from supermarkets)

7 to 9 cups peanut oil, to fry

Hot Fudge Sauce (page 198) or store-bought hot fudge sauce, warmed

Line a baking sheet that will fit in your freezer with waxed paper.

Place the chopped peanuts in a deep, wide-mouthed bowl. Working quickly, using a number 8 (½-cup) ice cream scoop or a metal ½-cup measuring cup, scoop out a ball of ice cream, then using two teaspoons to guide it, roll it in the chopped peanuts until evenly coated and transfer it to the prepared baking sheet. Repeat the process until you have 6 balls total. Freeze for at least 3 hours, preferably overnight, or until hard.

Place the eggs in a deep, wide-mouthed bowl and whisk them until well blended. Place the crushed vanilla wafers in another deep, wide-mouthed bowl. Working quickly, using two teaspoons to guide it, dip each frozen peanut-coated ball in the beaten eggs to coat evenly, then roll in the crushed wafers, making sure that each ball is completely covered. Freeze the balls again for at least 3 hours, preferably overnight, or until hard.

When you are ready to serve, place a wire rack on a paper towel-lined baking sheet and place it near the stove. Pour the oil into a medium (4- to 6-quart) cast-iron Dutch oven to a depth of 3 inches and set over medium-high heat. Heat the oil until a deep-fry thermometer registers 375F (190C).

Fry the balls in two batches (do not crowd the Dutch oven), 3 per batch, turning them often, until the coating just becomes crisp and golden brown, 10 to 20 seconds. Watch carefully because holes will burst in the sides if overcooked.

Working quickly, using a slotted spoon, transfer the balls to the prepared wire rack to drain until both batches are ready. Serve at once with the Hot Fudge Sauce.

CRANBERRY-ALMOND TART

Makes 6 servings

COMMERCIAL CRANBERRY SAUCE, AVAILABLE CANNED at supermarkets, sometimes titled a "relish" on the can label, is very thick and spreadable and makes for a quick topping. The tart-sweet flavor of the topping is a sensational contrast to the sweet filling and almond crust. Countrified, manly cast-iron cookware can certainly turn out some upscale goodies like this uptown tart, which is a good choice for the Christmas holiday table.

2 teaspoons butter, to grease

CRUST

1½ cups all-purpose flour

2 tablespoons sugar

¼ teaspoon salt

10 tablespoons unsalted butter, cut into ½-inch cubes, chilled

½ cup sliced almonds (2 ounces), toasted

1 tablespoon chilled water mixed with 1 teaspoon pure almond extract

FILLING

2 large eggs

½ cup sugar

1 cup sour cream

1 teaspoon pure vanilla extract

¼ teaspoon salt

1 (16-ounce) can whole-berry cranberry sauce, such as the Ocean Spray brand

Preheat the oven to 350F (175C). Line a 10-inch cast-iron skillet with foil, letting the ends extend over the sides. Grease the bottom and sides of the foil with the 2 teaspoons butter.

TO PREPARE THE CRUST: Combine the flour, sugar, and salt in a medium bowl and stir with a fork until well blended. Using a pastry blender or fork, cut in the butter until mixture resembles coarse crumbs.

Stir in the almonds (they will break up). Add the water-extract mixture and stir just until the dough comes together.

Transfer the dough to a lightly floured work surface and knead the dough briefly just until completely blended. Shape the dough into a disk, cover with waxed paper, then plastic wrap, and refrigerate at least 2 hours, preferably overnight, before rolling out.

Sandwich the dough disk between 2 sheets of waxed paper and roll out the dough into a circle that is 12 inches in diameter and ¼ inch thick. Using a small, sharp knife, trim off the ragged edges.

Line the prepared skillet with the dough, peeling off and discarding the waxed paper. Crimp the edges of the dough and bake the shell with pie weights or dried beans for 20 minutes. Remove the weights and bake until the shell is crisp but not browned, 3 to 4 minutes more.

MEANWHILE, MAKE THE FILLING: Combine all the filling ingredients except the cranberry sauce in a medium bowl and stir together until well blended. Pour into the baked tart shell (it should be about half full) and smooth the surface. Bake for 20 to 30 minutes or just until set; it should not brown.

Let cool in the skillet on a wire rack. Using the foil as handles, carefully lift the tart out of the skillet onto a serving platter. Carefully peel off, remove, and discard the foil. Spread the cranberry sauce over the tart in an even layer. Cover and refrigerate until ready to serve. Serve chilled or at room temperature.

APPLE DESSERT DUMPLINGS WITH CINNAMON ICE CREAM

Makes 4 servings

SOUL-WARMING BAKED APPLES IN A shroud of light biscuit pastry become extravagant when joined by homemade Cinnamon Ice Cream.

> 3 cups all-purpose flour
>
> 1 teaspoon salt
>
> 1 teaspoon sugar
>
> 2 tablespoons baking powder
>
> 1 cup solid vegetable shortening
>
> 1⅓ cups buttermilk
>
> 1 tablespoon unsalted butter, to grease
>
> 2 McIntosh, Granny Smith, or Gala apples
>
> 1 large egg yolk whisked with 2 tablespoons cold water, for egg wash
>
> Cinnamon Ice Cream (see below), to serve

Sift together the flour, salt, sugar, and baking powder into a medium bowl. Using a pastry blender or fork, cut in the shortening until the mixture resembles coarse crumbs. Stir in the buttermilk until well blended.

Knead the dough briefly on a lightly floured work surface, just until smooth. Roll the dough out to ¼-inch thickness. Cut the dough into 4 squares of the same size, trimming the edges to make them neat. Cover with a kitchen towel and reserve until ready to use.

Preheat the oven to 375F (190C). Liberally grease a 10-inch cast-iron skillet with the butter.

Peel, core, and halve each apple. Arrange each apple half, cavity side down, on the center of each dough square. Working quickly, brush the edges of the dough with the egg wash. Bring the corners of each dough square up, gathering the edges of the dough up and around the apple and gently press the edges together to seal firmly to make a round package that looks like a ball. (You can gently pick up each dumpling to press the dough; the egg wash will act like a glue.)

Brush the surface of each dumpling with more of the egg wash to help it brown nicely, and set the dumplings with sides touching in the prepared skillet.

Bake the dumplings on the center rack for 25 to 35 minutes, or until the crust is lightly golden brown and crisp. Serve at once with Cinnamon Ice Cream.

CINNAMON ICE CREAM

Makes 2 quarts

THIS ICE CREAM IS ALMOST buttery on the tongue. I call for cinnamon stick (which is Indonesian cinnamon), available at the supermarket, and then a second variety of cinnamon, a rare type, for the ground: Vietnamese cinnamon. The Vietnamese cinnamon is sweeter, more powerful, and more aromatic, and using both together has stupendous results. Vietnamese cinnamon is available from King Arthur Flour, The Baker's Catalogue, 1-800-827-6836 or http://www.kingarthurflour.com. Use a new wooden or stainless steel spoon to stir the ice cream base because the flavors embedded in an old wooden spoon could otherwise impart the cream with a displeasing flavor, resulting not in the superb ice cream you'll get otherwise. The ice cream machine I use is the very best; it's the White Mountain Ice Cream Freezer, which is an old-fashioned ice cream freezer complete with cast-iron mechanisms, and can be purchased on the Internet; just do a search of the words "White Mountain Ice Cream Freezer" to find a website shop.

5½ cups heavy cream

1 (3½-inch-long) cinnamon stick

1¼ cups sugar

4 large egg yolks, beaten

2 teaspoons pure vanilla extract

2 tablespoons ground cinnamon, preferably Vietnamese cinnamon

In a 2- to 3-quart saucepan over low heat, combine 3½ cups of the heavy cream and the cinnamon stick. Heat, stirring often, until scalded (you will see steam rise and bubbles will form around the edges; do boil), about 5 minutes. Remove and discard any skin from the surface of the scalded cream. Remove the pan from the heat, cover, and let stand for 1 hour for the cinnamon flavor to infuse the cream further.

In a large bowl, combine ¾ cup of the sugar and the egg yolks with an electric mixer. Beat on medium speed until the mixture is light colored and thick enough to form a broad ribbon when the beater is lifted, about 3 minutes.

Remove the cinnamon stick from the reserved cream mixture, squeeze out into the cream, and discard the cinnamon stick. Set the pan over low heat. Heat, stirring often, until hot but not boiling, 5 minutes.

Gradually pour the hot cream mixture into the egg yolk mixture in a thin, steady stream while beating on medium speed, just until blended.

Transfer the custard mixture along with the remaining ½ cup sugar to the top pan of a double boiler set over simmering water over medium-low heat. Simmer, stirring constantly, until thick enough to lightly coat the back of a wooden spoon, but do not allow the mixture to boil, 15 to 20 minutes.

Remove double boiler from the heat and strain the custard mixture through a fine-meshed metal sieve into a large heatproof bowl. Stir in the vanilla and let cool to room temperature. Place a sheet of plastic wrap directly on the surface of the mixture (so it does not form a skin) and chill overnight.

Just before making the ice cream, whisk the remaining 2 cups heavy cream and the ground cinnamon into the custard mixture until well blended.

Pour the mixture into a 4-quart ice cream maker and freeze according to manufacturer's instructions. The ice cream will be soft but ready to eat. Or transfer the soft ice cream to an air-tight container and freeze for 4 to 6 hours before serving to allow the ice cream to become semi-firm.

CHOCOLATE FUDGE SNACK CAKE

Makes 6 servings

I'VE ALWAYS WONDERED WHY NO one ever uses the common and yummy chocolate syrup (available at supermarkets) as a baking shortcut. I use it for a quick, not-fancy, home-style, single-layer, moist chocolate cake.

1 tablespoon butter, to grease

1 tablespoon unsweetened cocoa powder, to dust

1 cup all-purpose flour

1 teaspoon baking powder

1 stick (½ cup) unsalted butter, at room temperature

1 cup sugar

4 large eggs

1 teaspoon pure vanilla extract

1 cup Hot Fudge Sauce (page 198) or 1 cup canned chocolate syrup, at room temperature

Confectioners' sugar, to dust

Preheat the oven to 350F (175C). Liberally grease the bottom and sides of a 10-inch cast-iron skillet with the 1 tablespoon butter, and dust it with the 1 tablespoon cocoa powder, gently shaking the skillet to remove any excess cocoa powder. Place on a baking sheet.

Sift the flour and baking powder together into a medium bowl.

In a medium bowl, beat the butter with an electric mixer on medium speed until creamy. Add the sugar and beat until light and fluffy, about 1 minute. Add the eggs, 1 at a time, beating thoroughly after each addition. Add the vanilla, then the sifted dry ingredients alternately with the fudge sauce, beating well after each addition, until well blended.

Pour the batter into the skillet. Bake in the center of the oven for 45 to 50 minutes or until a cake tester or toothpick inserted 1 inch from the center comes out almost clean with a few moist crumbs clinging to it.

Cool the cake in the skillet on a wire rack for 5 minutes. Run a small, sharp knife around the cake edge to loosen the sides from the skillet, then invert the cake onto a serving platter. Once the cake is cool, sift with confectioners' sugar over the top and serve.

CHOCOLATE MUFFINS WITH CHOCOLATE CHEESECAKE TOPPING

Makes 1½ dozen muffins

THESE MUFFINS ARE RICH ENOUGH that I dare call them "cupcakes." Whether you serve them for breakfast, brunch, or dessert, you'll love them.

MUFFINS

> 2 cups all-purpose flour
>
> ¾ cup unsweetened cocoa powder
>
> 1¼ cups sugar
>
> 1 tablespoon baking powder
>
> ½ teaspoon baking soda
>
> ½ teaspoon salt
>
> 2 large eggs
>
> 1 cup buttermilk
>
> 1 stick (½ cup) unsalted butter, melted
>
> 1 teaspoon pure vanilla extract

CHOCOLATE CHEESECAKE TOPPING

> 2 (8-ounce) containers Kraft Philadelphia Flavors Cheesecake Flavor Cream Cheese Spread (available at supermarkets)
>
> 1 cup confectioners' sugar, sifted
>
> ⅛ cup unsweetened cocoa powder

TO MAKE THE MUFFINS: Preheat the oven to 400F (205C). Line 2 (12-cup) cast-iron muffin pans with fluted paper cupcake liners.

Sift together the flour, cocoa, sugar, baking powder, baking soda, and salt into a large bowl.

In a medium bowl, whisk together the eggs, buttermilk, butter, and vanilla until well blended. Pour the liquid mixture into the bowl with the dry ingredients. Stir together just until mixture is well blended; do not overmix.

Spoon the batter into the prepared muffin cups, filling the cups three-quarters full. Fill any unused cups halfway with water.

Bake for 15 to 20 minutes or until a cake tester or toothpick inserted in the center comes out almost clean with a few moist crumbs clinging to it.

Remove from the oven and let the muffins cool to room temperature in the pans on a wire rack.

MEANWHILE, TO MAKE THE TOPPING: Combine the cream cheese spread, confectioners' sugar, and cocoa powder in a large bowl. Using a fork, stir vigorously until well blended and smooth. Cover and refrigerate until ready to serve. Frost muffins with topping and serve.

CHOCOLATE LOVERS' DESSERT PIZZA

I'VE GONE A LITTLE CRAZY before and made marzipan "pepperoni," "mushroom," and "bell pepper" slices on top of "tomato sauce" (raspberry preserves), complete with "mozzarella cheese" slices (made from white chocolate). But I thought that a little too time-consuming, so here is another version of this killer pizza, which is really a thin chocolate confection with a deep chocolate glaze.

CAKE

   1 cup (2 sticks) unsalted butter, at room temperature

   1¼ cups sugar

   6 large eggs, beaten

   ½ cup unsweetened cocoa powder

   3 ounces semisweet chocolate, melted and cooled

TOPPING

   3 ounces sweet chocolate, finely chopped

   ½ cup water

   6 tablespoons unsalted butter

   3 tablespoons vegetable oil

   ¾ cup unsweetened cocoa powder

   1 cup confectioners' sugar

   2 (11-ounce) cans mandarin orange segments, drained (available from supermarkets)

TO PREPARE THE CAKE: Preheat the oven to 325F (165C). Line a 12-inch cast-iron skillet with foil, letting the edges of the foil extend over the skillet sides. Coat the foil with nonstick cooking spray.

   In a medium bowl, combine the butter and sugar. Beat the mixture with an electric mixer on medium speed until light and fluffy, about 2 minutes.

   Reduce the speed to low and beat in the eggs just until blended, scraping down the sides of the bowl with a rubber spatula. Add the cocoa and chocolate and beat on medium speed, scraping down the sides of the bowl, until well blended and smooth, about 2 minutes.

Pour the batter into the prepared skillet and smooth the surface. Bake for 40 to 50 minutes, or until the cake springs back when lightly touched and a cake tester or toothpick inserted in the center comes out clean with a few dry crumbs clinging to it. (The cake will have a thin, crusty surface and will feel soft but will firm when cooled.) Transfer the cake to a wire rack and let cool in the skillet to room temperature.

TO MAKE THE TOPPING: Combine the chocolate, water, butter, and vegetable oil in the upper pan of a double boiler, with the bottom pan partially filled with simmering water over medium heat. Heat the mixture, stirring, until the chocolate and butter melts and the mixture is smooth and well blended.

Remove from the heat. Whisk in the cocoa and confectioners' sugar until well blended and smooth. Remove the top pan from the bottom, and let cool at room temperature until the glaze is thickened, but still pourable, about 10 minutes.

TO ASSEMBLE THE PIZZA: Using the foil as handles, remove the cooled cake from the skillet, then carefully invert it onto a serving platter (so the cake does not break). Slowly peel off and discard the foil from the cake.

Pour the cooled glaze over the top of the pizza, using a knife to spread evenly and allowing it to drip over the edges onto the serving platter. Arrange the mandarin orange slices in a decorative pattern on top and serve.

WARM CHOCOLATE
BLACK BREAD PUDDING

OFTEN BREAD PUDDINGS ARE BAKED with the pan inserted in a water bath, but this confection works well baked in a cast-iron skillet. You can substitute another bread that is taste-compatible with chocolate, such as Challah bread or a French baguette, but then of course it can't be called a "black bread" pudding. Sometimes I combine both a black and white bread, which works quite nicely!

 5 cups 1-inch pumpernickel bread cubes, crusts removed

 6 large egg yolks

 3 large eggs

 1 teaspoon pure vanilla extract

 2 cups heavy cream

 2 cups milk

 ½ cup sugar

 10 ounces semisweet chocolate, finely chopped

 Fresh berries, to serve (optional)

 Whipped cream, to serve (optional)

Preheat the oven to 350F (175C). Coat a 10-inch cast-iron skillet with nonstick cooking spray. Place the bread cubes in the skillet and set aside. Place the skillet on a baking sheet.

Combine the egg yolks, eggs, and vanilla in a medium bowl and whisk until well blended. Set aside.

Combine the cream, milk, and sugar in a 2- to 3-quart saucepan over medium-low heat and cook, whisking often, until scalded (you will see steam rise and bubbles will form around the edges; do not boil), about 5 minutes.

Remove and discard any skin from the surface of the scalded mixture.

Stir in the chocolate and cook, whisking, until the chocolate is melted and the mixture well blended, about 2 minutes. Gradually pour in the reserved egg mixture in a slow, steady stream while whisking; cook for 2 minutes.

Pour the chocolate custard over the bread in the skillet, pressing the bread down until submerged in the chocolate custard.

Bake in the center of the oven for 50 to 60 minutes, or until a cake tester or toothpick inserted in the center comes out almost clean with a few moist crumbs clinging to it. Let stand for 5 minutes in the skillet on a wire rack and serve warm with fresh berries and whipped cream.

LEMON-CARDAMOM CAKE

Makes 1 (9 × 5-inch) loaf; 6 servings

THE EXOTIC FLAVOR OF CARDAMOM with its lemony overtone lends this cake its Scandinavian mystique. I have been able to purchase ground cardamom at well-stocked supermarkets. If you are unable to purchase ground cardamom, you can prepare it at home from loose cardamom seeds available at Indian grocery stores. Alternatively, you can purchase cardamom pods and remove the seeds from the pods before grinding the seeds in an electric spice grinder until finely ground.

CAKE

1½ cups all-purpose flour

1 teaspoon baking powder

¼ teaspoon salt

6 tablespoons unsalted butter, at room temperature

1 cup sugar

2 large eggs

Grated zest of 1 medium lemon

½ cup buttermilk

1 teaspoon finely ground cardamom

GLAZE

1 cup confectioners' sugar

1 tablespoon milk

½ teaspoon pure lemon extract

Grated zest of 1 medium lemon

TO MAKE THE CAKE: Preheat the oven to 350F (175C). Coat a 9 × 5-inch cast-iron loaf pan with nonstick cooking spray.

Sift the flour, baking powder, and salt into a medium bowl and reserve.

In the large bowl, beat the butter and sugar with an electric mixer on medium speed until light and fluffy, about 3 minutes. Beat in the eggs, 1 at a time, then the lemon zest, buttermilk, and cardamom. On low speed, blend in the reserved flour mixture just until combined; do not overmix.

Spoon batter into prepared pan, smoothing the surface. Bake in the center of the oven for 35 to 40 minutes or until a cake tester or toothpick inserted 1 inch from the center comes out almost clean with a few moist crumbs clinging to it.

Transfer the cake to a wire rack and let cool in the pan to room temperature.

MEANWHILE, TO PREPARE THE GLAZE: Stir together the glaze ingredients in a small bowl until well blended. Remove the cake from the pan and spread the glaze on the top of the cake and serve.

BLUEBERRY BUCKLE
WITH ALMOND CRUMB TOPPING

THIS CLASSIC AMERICAN DESSERT "BUCKLES" as it bakes, hence its name. It's the kind of dessert you wish you could still find at local bake sales, but now you can make it at home.

BLUEBERRY MIXTURE

> 2 tablespoons butter, to grease
>
> 2 tablespoons all-purpose flour, to dust
>
> ⅓ cup sugar
>
> 2 sticks (1 cup) unsalted butter, at room temperature
>
> 1 large egg, beaten
>
> 2 cups all-purpose flour
>
> 1 teaspoon baking powder
>
> 1 teaspoon baking soda
>
> 1 cup buttermilk, divided
>
> 4 cups fresh blueberries, mixed with ¼ to ½ cup sugar (depending on the sweetness of the blueberries)

TOPPING

> ½ cup sugar
>
> ½ cup firmly packed light brown sugar
>
> 1 cup all-purpose flour
>
> ½ teaspoon ground nutmeg
>
> ¼ teaspoon pure almond extract
>
> 1 stick (½ cup) unsalted butter, at room temperature
>
> 1 (2.25-ounce) package sliced almonds (½ cup total), toasted, finely chopped

TO PREPARE THE BLUEBERRY MIXTURE: Preheat the oven to 350F (175C). Liberally grease the bottom and sides of a 12-inch cast-iron skillet with the 2 tablespoons butter and dust it with the 2 tablespoons flour, gently shaking the skillet to remove any excess flour.

In a large bowl, beat the sugar with the 2 sticks butter with an electric mixer on medium speed until light and fluffy, about 3 minutes. Beat in the egg just until blended.

Sift together the 2 cups flour with the baking powder and baking soda into a large bowl. Add half of the flour mixture to the butter mixture and beat until well blended, 1 minute. Beat in half the buttermilk until well blended. Beat in the remaining flour mixture and remaining buttermilk, beating after each addition until well blended.

Spread the batter evenly into the prepared skillet and sprinkle the blueberries evenly over all.

To make the topping: Combine all the topping ingredients in a medium bowl. Working quickly, work the mixture in between your fingertips to blend and form large crumbs. Sprinkle the topping evenly over the blueberries. Press three fingers through the topping about halfway down into the batter in 6 different places or until the buckle looks bumpy.

Bake for 50 to 60 minutes on the center oven rack or until golden brown and a cake tester or toothpick inserted 1 inch from the center comes out almost clean with a few moist crumbs clinging to it.

Let stand in the skillet on a wire rack for 5 minutes. Serve warm directly from the skillet.

WILD BLACKBERRY COBBLER

Makes 4 servings

YOU CAN ALSO MAKE THIS cobbler substituting raspberries for the blackberries (both berries are now readily available at supermarkets). If you use raspberries, use ground cinnamon in place of the nutmeg. The cobbler is delicious with blackberry ice cream or sorbet, both often available at the supermarket. I also find that serving it with vanilla ice cream or lemon sorbet provides an amazing taste seduction.

1 cup plus 2 tablespoons all-purpose flour

¾ cup plus 2 teaspoons sugar, or to taste

1½ teaspoons baking powder

½ teaspoon ground nutmeg

¼ teaspoon salt

5 tablespoons unsalted butter, cut into ½-inch cubes, chilled, divided

1 teaspoon pure vanilla extract

⅓ cup heavy cream, chilled

5 cups fresh blackberries

¼ cup water

Blackberry or vanilla ice cream, to serve

Preheat the oven to 400F (205C). Using a fork, stir together the 2 tablespoons flour and the ¾ cup sugar in a small bowl until well blended, then reserve.

Into a medium mixing bowl, sift together the remaining 1 cup flour, remaining 2 teaspoons sugar, baking powder, nutmeg, and salt. Using a pastry blender or fork, cut in 3 tablespoons of the butter until the mixture resembles coarse crumbs. Stir the vanilla into the cream and then stir it into the flour mixture just until the mixture is well blended and gathers together to form a dough.

Using your hands, form the dough into 8 equal-size biscuits, but do not overwork the dough. Set aside until ready to use.

Combine the blackberries and water in a stainless steel 2-to 3-quart saucepan and place over medium heat. Cook, stirring occasionally, until the blackberries begin to fall apart and the mixture comes to a full boil, about 5 minutes.

Stir in the reserved flour-sugar mixture until well blended. Taste and add more sugar if necessary for desired sweetness. Cook, stirring occasionally, until the mixture has thickened but remains glossy, about 4 minutes more. Remove from the heat and pour mixture into a 9-inch cast-iron skillet.

Dot the remaining 2 tablespoons butter over the blackberries. Place the reserved biscuits, evenly spaced, but not touching one another, in a circle formation with one biscuit in the center of the circle over the blackberries.

Bake for 20 to 25 minutes or until the biscuits are a delicate golden brown and the cobbler is bubbling.

Let stand for 5 minutes in the skillet on a wire rack. Serve warm directly from the skillet with blackberry or vanilla ice cream.

STRAWBERRY CREAM STACK CAKE

Makes 1 (8-inch, 4-layer) cake; 4 to 6 servings

IF YOU'RE NOT FAMILIAR WITH a "stack cake," picture a tower of large, soft cookies each with a crisp crust and a fruit filling in between the layers. I have heard many stories as to its origin, but the tale I like best is that during pioneer times, it was a traditional wedding cake (the filling often made with dried apples), and each guest would bring a layer to be "stacked" at the reception.

FILLING

> 2 pounds fresh strawberries, thinly sliced (about 8 cups)
>
> 2 to 2½ cups sugar (depending on the sweetness of the strawberries)
>
> 1 tablespoon fresh lemon juice

CAKE

> 3 cups all-purpose flour
>
> ½ teaspoon baking soda
>
> 1 teaspoon ground allspice
>
> ½ teaspoon ground ginger
>
> 1 stick (½ cup) unsalted butter, at room temperature
>
> ½ cup sugar
>
> ¼ cup molasses
>
> 1 large egg, at room temperature
>
> 2 tablespoons buttermilk, at room temperature
>
> Confectioners' sugar, to garnish
>
> 2 cups thinly sliced fresh strawberries, to garnish
>
> Vanilla Whipped Cream (page 195), to serve

TO MAKE THE FILLING: Combine the filling ingredients in a heavy 3- to 4-quart pot, stir until well blended, and place over medium heat. Cook, stirring often, until the sugar dissolves, 3 minutes. Increase the heat to high and bring to a boil. Boil until the mixture is as thick as jam, stirring often, 10 to 15 minutes. (Mixture will thicken more as it cools but will still be pourable.)

Meanwhile, to make the cake: Preheat the oven to 350F (175C). Sift together the flour, baking soda, allspice, and ginger into a large bowl and set aside.

Beat the butter and sugar in a large bowl with an electric mixer on medium speed until light and fluffy, 3 minutes. Beat in the molasses, egg, and buttermilk just until blended. Using a rubber spatula, fold the reserved dry ingredients into the wet ingredients until well blended and a dough forms.

Turn the dough out onto a lightly floured work surface. Divide the dough into 4 equal portions. Using the outline of an 8-inch round baking pan, draw a circle on parchment paper. Roll out 1 portion of the dough to fit the circle, then fit the dough circle and the parchment paper onto the bottom of the 10-inch cast-iron skillet.

Bake in the center of the oven for 10 to 12 minutes or until the cake layer surface is crisp like a cookie.

With the help of a large, wide spatula, gently (so as not to break the cake layer) slide the cake layer off of the skillet onto a wire rack. While the cake layer is still warm, slide the parchment paper out from under the cake layer so you can re-use the parchment paper for the remaining 3 cake layers.

Repeat the process with the remaining dough for a total of 4 baked cake layers. Allow the cake layers to cool completely on the wire rack.

To assemble the cake: Place 1 cooled cake layer onto a serving platter and ladle each layer with one-third of the filling, allowing the filling to spread across the cake layer. Repeat with remaining filling, not spreading any filling on the top layer. (Use a large serving platter, as the filling will ooze and surround the cake for a pretty presentation.)

Just before serving, dust the top of the cake with confectioners' sugar, then scatter the fresh strawberries over the top, allowing a few to fall onto the platter. Use a serrated knife to cut into wedges and serve at once so the cake layers are moist from the filling but aren't allowed to become soggy. Pass a chilled bowl of the Vanilla Whipped Cream to serve on the side.

MINCEMEAT TURNOVERS

OLD-TIME MINCEMEAT INCLUDED MINCED MEAT (most often beef), which is how it derived its name. Nowadays, this concoction is made of all the ingredients—without the meat—an assortment of candied fruits, spices, beef suet, and brandy.

1½ cups all-purpose flour

½ cup cake flour

1 teaspoon salt

2 tablespoons sugar

½ cup cream cheese (4 ounces), at room temperature

6 to 10 tablespoons chilled water, as needed

2 teaspoons butter, to grease

1⅓ cups homemade or store-bought mincemeat

Confectioners' sugar, to dust

In a large bowl, sift together the flours, salt, and sugar. Using a pastry blender or fork, cut in the cream cheese until the mixture resembles coarse crumbs. Add the chilled water, 1 table-spoon at a time, and stir with a fork until the dough gathers into a ball but is not sticky. Do not overwork the dough. Form into a disk, wrap in waxed paper, then plastic wrap and refrigerate for at least 1 hour or overnight.

Remove the chilled dough from the refrigerator and let sit at room temperature for 5 minutes. On a lightly floured work surface, roll out the dough to ¼-inch thickness. Using a 6-inch-diameter bowl as a guide, using a pastry wheel or small, sharp knife, cut out 4 rounds of dough, re-rolling the dough scraps if needed.

Preheat the oven to 350F (175C). Lightly grease a 12-inch cast-iron skillet with the butter.

Place about ⅓ cup of mincemeat on half of each round about 1 inch from the edge. Dip your fingers in water and, working with one turnover at a time, wet the edges of dough round with water. Form a turnover by folding one half over the filling, and using your fingers, pressing the edges together. Seal by pressing the flat tines of a fork along the edges. Repeat with remaining rounds and mincemeat.

Cut 3 small diagonal slits in the top of each turnover for steam vents and transfer to the prepared skillet. Refrigerate for 1 hour.

Bake in the 350F (175C) oven for 35 to 45 minutes or until the edges are lightly golden brown and the crust crisp.

Transfer to a wire rack and let stand for 5 minutes. Sift with confectioners' sugar to dust and serve warm.

Metric Conversion Charts

Comparison to Metric Measure

When You Know	Symbol	Multiply By	To Find	Symbol
teaspoons	tsp.	5.0	milliliters	ml
tablespoons	tbsp.	15.0	milliliters	ml
fluid ounces	fl. oz.	30.0	milliliters	ml
cups	c	0.24	liters	l
pints	pt.	0.47	liters	l
quarts	qt.	0.95	liters	l
ounces	oz.	28.0	grams	g
pounds	lb.	0.45	kilograms	kg
Fahrenheit	F	5/9 (after subtracting 32)	Celsius	C

Fahrenheit to Celsius

F	C
200–205	95
220–225	105
245–250	120
275	135
300–305	150
325–330	165
345–350	175
370–375	190
400–405	205
425–430	220
445–450	230
470–475	245
500	260

Liquid Measure to Milliliters

¼	teaspoon	=	1.25	milliliters
½	teaspoon	=	2.5	mililiters
¾	teaspoon	=	3.75	milliliters
1	teaspoon	=	5.0	milliliters
1-¼	teaspoons	=	6.25	milliliters
1-½	teaspoons	=	7.5	milliliters
1-¾	teaspoons	=	8.75	milliliters
2	teaspoons	=	10.0	milliliters
1	tablespoon	=	15.0	milliliters
2	tablespoons	=	30.0	milliliters

Liquid Measure to Liters

¼	cup	=	0.06	liters
½	cup	=	0.12	liters
¾	cup	=	0.18	liters
1	cup	=	0.24	liters
1-¼	cups	=	0.3	liters
1-½	cups	=	0.36	liters
2	cups	=	0.48	liters
2-½	cups	=	0.6	liters
3	cups	=	0.72	liters
3-½	cups	=	0.84	liters
4	cups	=	0.96	liters
4-½	cups	=	1.08	liters
5	cups	=	1.2	liters
5-½	cups	=	1.32	liters

INDEX

Mara Reid Rogers, CCP, is an award-winning author, media personality, and culinary/home-entertaining expert with a national presence. She is the culinary expert and co-host of the radio show *The Midday Dish with Mara Reid Rogers* on WJON-AM. Prior to that, the host and executive producer of the lifestyle radio show *Gracious Living Today* on WQXI-AM (Georgia). She was co-host of the National Public television series *Cook-Off America* that was one of the top three cooking shows in the nation.

Rogers was a contributing food writer and food and prop stylist to the largest newspaper in the Southeast: The Atlanta *Journal and Constitution*, as well as a former assistant food and entertaining editor for *House Beautiful*. She was also former food and entertaining editor for Atlanta *Homes and Lifestyles* magazine, where she wrote main features and restaurant reviews.

Mara's site, http://www.cyberhomechef.com (where she is known as "The Cyber Home Chef") brings the world of creative home cooking to computers. Within two months of launching her site, she won several awards, among them the national *Usa Today* Hot Site Award.

Rogers is a prolific cookbook author. *The South the Beautiful Cookbook*, which she co-authored, was lauded (the year it was published) as "One Of The Year's Top Ten Cookbooks" according to Nation's Restaurant News. She is a trend-forecaster and helps companies sell their products through her monitoring of trends. She has been profiled in many areas of the United States in print, television, Internet, and radio, and is experienced in media venues ranging from satellite media tours to web site forums, and QVC. She's been the national spokesperson for several major companies.

A graduate of the professional culinary program offered by Peter Kump's New York Cooking School, Rogers has also earned the prestigious classification of Certified Culinary Professional (CCP). She also has a degree in commercial photography and communication design from Parsons School of Design in New York City, and concentrated writing studies from Hampshire College in Amherst, Massachusetts.